STORIES IN HISTORY

HOW AMERICA GREW

1775–1914 GREW

nextext

Table of Contents

Under the leadership of Daniel Boone, a team of 28 woodsmen cut a road over the Appalachian Mountains. One of the woodsmen tells what it was like to be part of the effort that opened up Kentucky and the West to settlement.

A retired steamboat captain tells a young visitor about the exciting days when rivers were America's best "highways" through the wilderness.

PART III: A WORLD POWER

About this Book

The stories are historical fiction. They are based on historical fact, but some of the characters and events may be fictional. In the Sources section, you'll learn which is which and where the information came from.

The illustrations are all historical. If they are from a time different from the story, the caption tells you. Original documents help you understand the time period. Maps let you know where things were.

Items explained in People and Terms to Know are repeated in the Glossary. Look there if you come across a name or term you don't know.

Historians do not always know or agree on the exact dates of events in the past. The letter c before a date means "about" (from the Latin word circa*).*

If you would like to read more about these exciting times, you will find recommendations in Reading on Your Own.

A pioneer father and son take a rest from clearing the trees around their log cabin. ▶

Background

"Go west, young man, and grow up with the country."
—Horace Greeley

In the 1780s, a string of 13 former colonies stretched along the Atlantic coast of North America. The next 100 years saw these colonies grow into a nation that reached from the Atlantic to the Pacific Ocean and beyond. People from all over the world traveled to the United States to seek riches, new farmland, and religious freedom. They also faced great challenges.

The Land

"After refreshing ourselves we proceeded on to the top of the dividing ridge from which I discovered immense ranges of high mountains still to the West of us with their tops partially covered with snow. . . . Here I first tasted the water of the great Columbia river."
—Meriwether Lewis, Aug. 12, 1805

Across the Appalachians

In the 1700s, the western boundary of the original colonies was formed by the Appalachian Mountains. They stretched nearly 2,000 miles from what is now Canada to Alabama. The rugged mountains and dense forests were hard to explore and settle.

The land between the Appalachians and the Mississippi River had once been claimed by both the French and British. The British drove the French out during the French and Indian War (1754–1763). British colonists then began to move westward.

In 1775, Daniel Boone and a crew of 28 men blazed a trail over the Appalachians. Boone's group built the Wilderness Road that led from eastern Virginia to Kentucky and beyond. The road opened the way for settlement. After the Revolution, it became the main route to the territories of the West.

▲
Lewis and Clark meet some Native Americans on the Columbia River.

Westward Expansion

In 1803, the United States wanted a port at the mouth of the Mississippi River. The land was owned by France, so President Thomas Jefferson sent James Monroe to France to buy New Orleans and West Florida. But the French wanted to sell *all* the land from the Mississippi River to the Rocky Mountains. Monroe agreed to pay $15 million for it. With the Louisiana Purchase, America doubled her territory—for about three cents an acre.

Jefferson immediately sent a team of explorers, headed by Meriwether Lewis and William Clark, into the new territory. From 1804 to 1806, the Lewis and Clark Expedition traveled up the Missouri River, across the Rocky Mountains, and down the Snake and Columbia Rivers to the Pacific Ocean. Along the way, they collected plants, animals, and mineral samples. They also made maps and wrote descriptions of the rich territory.

Other adventurers were also drawn to the Louisiana Territory. They included French, Spanish, and American mountain men who trapped beavers and sold their furs and often served as scouts and guides for explorers and settlers.

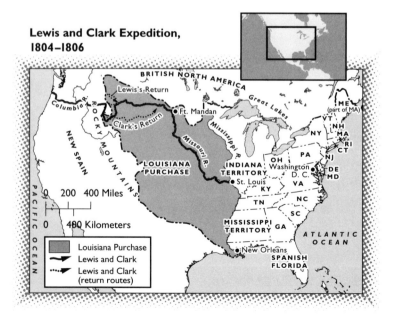

Lewis and Clark Expedition, 1804–1806

Texas and California

Mexico once included the land that today stretches from Texas to California and includes Utah, Nevada, New Mexico, and Arizona. The Mexican government wanted Americans to settle in Texas and help them fight against Indian raiders. They hoped that if Americans lived in Texas, the U. S. government would not try to take it by force. So they offered cheap land and no taxes to bring in new settlers.

Their plan worked too well. By the 1830s, there were many more Americans than Mexicans in Texas. Problems arose between the Mexican government and the American settlers that led to the Texas Revolution.

After a number of defeats, including a famous one at a mission called the Alamo, the Americans soundly defeated the Mexicans. A treaty was signed, and a new country, The Republic of Texas, was established in 1839. In separate treaties in 1848 and 1853, Mexico sold its other areas in the Southwest to the United States for about $28 million. The United States now owned land from ocean to ocean.

The Price of Growth

"When I was young, I walked all over this country, east and west, and saw no other people than the Apaches. After many summers I walked again and found another race of people had come to take it."
—Apache leader Cochise (c. 1812–1874)

The Indian Removal

Before 1810, Thomas Jefferson and others hoped that Indians who lived east of the Mississippi would become farmers and blend into American society. Many in the Southeast—such as the Seminole, Cherokee, Choctaw, and Creek—gave up hunting and became farmers.

The Cherokee built towns and started schools. They created a constitution similar to the U.S. Constitution. They developed a written language that is still in use today. Eventually, Indian groups of the Southeast lived on millions of acres of rich farmland.

Settlers began to see the Indians as competitors for valuable farmland and conflicts between whites and Indians were more and more frequent. By 1820, settlers called for all Indians to be "removed" to land west of the Mississippi. President Andrew Jackson said that removal of the Indians was for their own protection.

In 1830, Congress passed the Indian Removal Act. This called for all Indians living east of the Mississippi River to be moved to Indian Territory in present-day Oklahoma. There, Jackson promised, "as long as grass grows and water runs, . . . [the land] will be yours forever."

Native Americans did not trust Jackson's promise. The Cherokee took the battle to court. They argued that they were a self-ruling nation and the United States had no legal power over them. In 1831, the Supreme Court ruled that Indian tribes were "domestic dependent nations." The Court said that Indians had to obey federal law, but they had none of the rights of U.S. citizens.

Many Indians refused to leave their homes and were removed by the army. Some, like the Seminole in Florida, chose to fight. Many were killed, and the rest were removed to Indian Territory.

Indians in the rest of the country were also forced onto reservations—frequently on land that no settlers wanted.

The Seminole leader Osceola and his people resisted being forced to leave their homeland in Florida.

▼

Slavery and the Growing Nation

During the mid-1800s, the United States was anything but united. People in the South depended on slaves to work their large fields. But slavery did not take hold in the North, where farms were smaller and fewer workers were needed. Some Northern states had made slavery illegal in the state constitutions they wrote right after the American Revolution. Many in the North wanted to end slavery, but Southern planters disagreed.

In 1848, there were thirty states. Fifteen states supported slavery, and fifteen opposed it. When a territory such as Texas or California asked for statehood, leaders in Congress based their votes on that territory's position on slavery. Because California was against slavery, Southern leaders refused to allow it into the Union. They were afraid California would tip the balance of voting in Congress. But in 1848, an event occurred that forced the acceptance of California into the Union. It also marked the beginning of the end of U.S. slavery.

United States, 1850

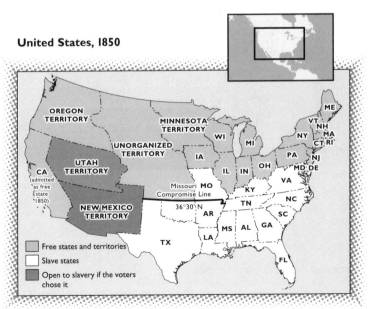

Why America Grew

"The news spreads that wonderful 'diggings' have been discovered. . . . [Men] rush vulture-like upon the scene . . . honestly and industriously commence digging for gold, and lo! as if a fairy's wand has been waved . . . a full-grown mining town hath sprung into existence."

—Louisa Smith Clappe

The Lure of Gold

Early in 1848, a carpenter building a sawmill near Coloma, California, found a few nuggets of gold in the American River, and the gold rush began. Over the next several years, tens of thousands of treasure-seekers traveled from the eastern United States to California. Some sailed around the tip of South America while others traveled 2,000 miles by wagon train across a harsh and challenging continent.

Before the discovery of gold, California had asked to be a territory. Now California demanded statehood. If statehood was not granted, California planned to form a separate country. The gleam of gold won out. California was granted statehood in 1850. The South agreed only on the condition that Northern states promised to return runaway slaves to their owners.

▲

The California Gold Rush was the first of many in the West. Here, miners pan for gold in North Dakota in the 1880s.

Over the next few years, differences between the Southern and Northern states grew worse, leading to the Civil War in 1861. In the late 1800s, a French writer put it this way: "It was the gold of California that gave the fatal blow to the institution of slavery in the United States."

Overland Trails

Gold wasn't the only reason settlers traveled westward. During the late 1700s and most of the 1800s, thousands of people went in search of a better life and rich farmland.

Settlers organized caravans of wagons. They often met at St. Louis, Missouri, or Independence,

Missouri. There they would form companies, elect officers, hire guides, and gather supplies. When the weather permitted, they set out on their long journey west. They faced rivers, mountains, and hostile Indians. The days were long and difficult. Travelers rose at 4 A.M. to eat and prepare to leave at 7 A.M. At about 4 P.M., they made camp, cooked, and grazed their animals, leaving little time to relax before bedtime.

One of the emigrants' worst fears on their journeys westward was the possibility of an Indian attack, such as the one shown in this engraving from 1857.

▼

During the 1800s, many famous wagon train roads developed—the Oregon and Mormon Trails in the North, the Santa Fe and Old Spanish Trails to California, and the Southern Overland Mail Trail through Texas to California.

Farmers and Ranchers

Farmers often traveled the Oregon Trail, heading for Oregon's rich Willamette Valley. One group of farmers, led by Brigham Young, settled in the Mexican territory of Utah. Settlement increased when Utah became a U.S. possession in 1848. As more people traveled westward, ranches and farms sprang up across the Great Plains to the Rocky Mountains and beyond.

Farmers who began by growing crops and raising cattle only for their own use soon began providing food for a growing nation. The transportation of food and other goods across the country created new problems.

Between 1867 and 1871, ranchers drove about 1.5 million head of cattle from Texas to the railroad in Kansas. From there, the cattle were sent by train to eastern markets. The long cattle drives ended when the railroads built branch lines in the late 1800s.

A World Power

*"A new consciousness seems to have come upon us—
the consciousness of strength—and with it a new appetite,
the yearning to show our strength. . . . taking
[our] place with the armed nations."*
—*Washington Post* editorial in June 1896

▲
Colonel Theodore Roosevelt and his Rough Riders pose for a picture after
the Battle of San Juan Hill on July 1, 1898.

Manifest Destiny

B y the 1840s, many Americans believed that it was the "manifest destiny" (that is, obvious future) of the United States to expand westward and fill the entire continent. Not all Americans supported this idea. Some argued that the United States had no right to take over land that already belonged to others. Others worried that the United States would become too large to govern itself well. Most Americans, however, were persuaded by the promise of land and opportunity.

By the end of the 1800s, the boundaries of the United States were settled. The nation joined other world powers in competing for trade and colonies. Those who believed in expansion insisted that the United States had a duty to spread its political system and the Christian religion to the rest of the world. Americans had once fought a revolution to escape colonial rule. Now the United States had its own colonies.

America in the Pacific and Caribbean

For many people, expansion was good economics. American businesses wanted more markets for their goods. They needed raw materials they could get only from other countries. American businesses expanded their markets into Asia, Africa, and Latin America. United States government officials began to insist that American interests needed to be protected by a strong navy. This navy would need to have bases overseas. The bases would be safe places for repairing and fueling ships. So the United States joined other nations in a race to take over islands in the Pacific.

Japan

Commodore Matthew Perry first went to Japan in 1853 to persuade the Japanese to trade with the United States. He returned the following year with seven warships. Perry also brought gifts and said he came in friendship, but Japan's rulers feared that the United States might seize their nation. So Japan's rulers agreed to allow Americans to do business with their people. At the same time, Japan improved its own industries and built its own army and navy.

Hawaii

Hawaii, in the middle of the Pacific Ocean, was a perfect location for naval bases and refueling stations. Other Americans went to Hawaii for different reasons. Some went to buy and sell crops. Others went to Hawaii to convert the "uncivilized" peoples to Christianity.

Cuba

Supporters of U.S. expansion had long been interested in Cuba, just 90 miles away from Florida in the Gulf of Mexico. They supported Cuba's fight for independence from Spain. This decision led to the Spanish-American War. Americans fought the Spanish in places as far away as the Philippine Islands in the Pacific Ocean.

Panama Canal

Now the United States had interests in both the Caribbean and the Pacific regions. It became important to try to cut the time and expense of traveling around the tip of South America. To do this, the government proposed digging a canal across Central America.

At that time, Panama belonged to Colombia. Colombia refused the offer of the United States to build the canal. Troops from Panama, with help from the United States, revolted against Colombia. They declared Panama an independent nation. In 1914, after ten years of construction, the first ship passed through the Panama Canal.

Time Line

1775—Wilderness Road built.

1804–1806—Lewis and Clark lead an expedition.

1825—Erie Canal completed.

1830—Congress passes the Indian Removal Act.

1836—Texas declares independence from Mexico.

1838—Cherokee travel the Trail of Tears.

1842—First wagon train travels over Oregon Trail.

1845—United States annexes Texas.

1846–1848—War fought against Mexico.

1848—Gold discovered in California.

1854—Japan opens ports to U.S. ships.

1860–1865—Civil War fought.

1862—Homestead Act passed.

1867—First cattle driven from Texas to Kansas.

1869—Transcontinental railroad completed.

1893—Queen Liliuokalani overthrown in Hawaii.

1898—Spanish-American War fought.

1914—Panama Canal completed.

The First Frontier

Daniel Boone Moves to Kentucky

BY WALTER HAZEN

I'd heard of **Daniel Boone**, of course. Everyone had. Until we got together at the **stockade** on the 10th of March, 1775, however, I'd never seen him.

I have to say I was impressed by his appearance. He was not a tall man, but he had a very powerful build. His shoulders and chest were broad and his arms and legs were large. He looked to me like he could whip a bear!

I was one of the axmen who answered Daniel's call to gather at the stockade. The company that had hired him was offering us good money for about a month of hard work. Our job was to cut a

---

People and Terms to Know

Daniel Boone—(1734–1820) pioneer and frontiersman famous for exploring Kentucky and blazing the trail that led settlers to the West.
stockade—fence of wooden stakes built for defense.

Daniel Boone leads settlers through the Cumberland Gap in this painting by

road through the mountains into **Kentucky**. This was a distance of about 250 miles. The road had to be wide enough for wagons to pass over. Once the road was finished, we were to build a fort to protect all the settlers that would follow.

The stockade where we met was 50 miles northwest of Sycamore Shoals. Daniel said that's where the **Transylvania Company** was about to sign an agreement with the Cherokee Indians. According to the agreement, the Indians would give up 200,000 acres of land. This land was between the Kentucky and Cumberland Rivers, on the west side of the Appalachian Mountains. The Cherokee would also agree to let us cut a road through the mountains leading to the **Cumberland Gap**. What would they get in return? Six wagonloads of trinkets, firearms, liquor, and woolen stuff!

People and Terms to Know

Kentucky—land west of the Appalachian Mountains. Originally part of Virginia, Kentucky became a state in 1792.

Transylvania Company—company founded for the purpose of buying land from the Cherokee and establishing Kentucky as the fourteenth colony. The attempt failed.

Cumberland Gap—opening or pass in the Cumberland Mountains where present-day Virginia, Kentucky, and Tennessee meet. It served as the gateway to the West in the late 1800s and early 1900s.

"Can you believe those Indians gave away all that land for six wagonloads of junk?" I later said to Tom Campbell, one of our axmen.

"Well" he drawled, "I think they were swayed by the guns and ammunition. Remember—they had just lost a fight with some neighboring tribes. They thought the firearms would help them even the score. Besides, I understand that the Indians who signed that agreement think they came out ahead, since they didn't really own the land they were 'selling.'"

Maybe that was true; maybe it wasn't. But I remember Daniel saying that not all of the Indians were in favor of the agreement. Quite a few felt they had been cheated. These "few" would later give us trouble along the trail.

Anyhow, we set out on the 10th of March, about a week before the agreement was actually signed. Because I had more education than all the other fellows, Dan'l (that's what we all called him) asked if I would keep a record of everything that happened. Naturally I agreed.

There were about 30 of us, including Dan'l's daughter Susannah and a slave woman. The women's job was to cook and keep camp for us. Susy Boone had just married one of our axmen, a tough Irishman named Will Hayes. It was a hard life, but Susy never complained. She was just as tough as her father.

Cutting the road through the wilderness had its ups and downs. On the east side of the mountains, we just widened some Indian paths that were already there. On the west side, we followed buffalo trails as much as possible. Still, we had a lot of cutting to do through thick forests.

Our group of axmen went in front of the main group, which was headed by **Judge Richard Henderson**. Our job was to blaze the trail. Then the judge would follow with packhorses and wagons loaded with food and ammunition.

To be sure, our job was sometimes difficult. We had to chop our way through trees, vines, and overhanging branches. We had to burn through dead brush and cut through thick cane plants. We also had to remove fallen trees and lay logs across **sinkholes** and creeks. The weather didn't make it any easier. This was late winter, and we had to deal with snow and freezing rain. Then, when we finally crossed the mountains and got down into the valleys, we had to slosh through mud. It was hard going all the way.

On March 22, after barely two weeks, we reached Cumberland Gap. We could see Kentucky down below. How pretty it looked!

We could see Kentucky down below. How pretty it looked!

"Did you ever see such a sight?" I asked my friend Tom.

"Well," he said, "I'm more interested in what's down there. I hear there's lots of deer, elk, and buffalo, just for the taking. One fellow who went there before with Dan'l told me the horses' legs were stained plumb up to the knees from galloping through the wild strawberries."

"You're joshing," I said. "Doesn't that sound a little far-fetched?"

"Not to me, it doesn't," Tom answered. "And here's another thing: they say the wild turkeys in Kentucky are so fat that when you shoot one, its skin busts wide open when it hits the ground!"

Well, turkeys weren't quite that plump in Kentucky, but, as we found out later, they weren't exactly skinny either. It was those turkeys I was thinking about when we had our first trouble with Indians.

Remember how I said that a lot of Indians didn't agree with selling the land in Kentucky? Well, they felt threatened by our being there. So they attacked us on March 25 and then again two days later. Several in our party were killed. On April 1, Dan'l sent a messenger to the main group with a note. He told them to hurry as fast as they could.

▲
The settlers at Boonesborough successfully fought off an Indian attack in 1778.

We were attacked again on April 4. By this time, we had reached the spot on the Kentucky River where Dan'l said we should build the fort. When the main group finally arrived, the Indian threat died down. The increase in our numbers was enough to scare them off for a while.

We built our fort, which, in time, was called Boonesborough. The road we cut through the mountains was called the Wilderness Road. Twenty-five years have passed since we finished it. I hear that more than 200,000 people have traveled the Wilderness Road on their way west. I'm mighty proud that I played a part in that great adventure.

QUESTIONS TO CONSIDER

1. Why did some of the Indians agree to sell the land in Kentucky?

2. Why did other Indians disagree about allowing the Americans to settle Kentucky?

3. Why was the work of Henderson and Boone important to U.S. history?

4. How long did it take Boone and company to reach Cumberland Gap?

5. When does this story take place? What was happening in American history at that time?

Constance and the Great Race

BY STEPHEN CURRIE

*In the 1820s, roads in the United States were so poor
that rivers served as the major "highways." Steamboats in
the early 1800s greatly improved the speed of river travel.
Rivers became centers of trade, and small river ports grew
into good-sized cities.*

*By present-day standards, steamboats were slow. They
usually traveled less than 12 miles an hour. But by the
standards of the time, they were very fast. Between the
1820s and the 1850s, steamboats ruled transportation
and business in the interior of the United States.*

*   *   *

Captain Snellings was terribly old, thought
Marjorie. Why, he must be over eighty, judging by
his stooped shoulders and bald head. This was

1875, so subtract eighty years . . . Well! The captain had probably been born before 1800. She felt honored to have made the man's acquaintance.

"What about a lemonade, my dear?" said the captain.

"Yes, please," replied Marjorie.

"Eh?" The captain cupped a hand to his ear.

"Yes, *please*," Marjorie repeated in a louder voice. Lemonade would be good. Hot days here in Elizabethtown were far hotter than they were back home in New England. The summer heat of the Ohio Valley shimmered around you in great bulky waves.

Ah, she loved the cool summers of New England. Marjorie's thoughts drifted to home and her chain of gentleman callers—Charles the student, Jared the soldier, Thomas the storekeeper. When a girl was sixteen, she thought with a smile, romance was always in the air.

"Here we are." Stumbling slightly, Captain Snellings handed Marjorie a crystal glass of lemonade. "You are Julia's cousin, yes? You're visiting from out of town, I hear."

Marjorie nodded. Julia, also sixteen, had intended to come to see the captain as well. But she'd had an unexpected gentleman caller. Romance came before visits to kindly old men. "And you were a steamboat captain, Julia tells me."

The old man nodded. "A wonderful life it was, too, on the rivers."

Marjorie delicately sipped her lemonade and thought of gentleman callers. "Wasn't it—lonely?"

"Lonely?" The old man looked up in surprise. "How could it have been lonely when I had *Constance*?"

And yet, she couldn't help thinking that it also sounded terribly—romantic.

Constance? Through the window Marjorie could see the slim ribbon that was the Ohio River. She imagined a dashing young Captain Snellings, drifting along the Ohio. Then she imagined his dear wife, Constance, traveling with him.

"Tell me about Constance," Marjorie begged. "Was she pretty?"

"She was a beauty." Captain Snellings sipped from his glass. "There'll never be another like my poor *Constance*." Sadly he shook his head.

"Poor Constance?" Marjorie's heart raced, and she dropped her voice to nearly a whisper. "Did she—die?"

She hoped not. That would be horrible. And yet, she couldn't help thinking that it also sounded terribly—romantic.

The captain seemed not to have heard. "Listen," he said, leaning forward, "and I'll tell you about my beloved *Constance* and the Great Race of '27."

*　　*　　*

"It all began," said Captain Snellings, "when Ephraim Chester challenged us to a race. He piloted the *New Albany* at the time. It was one of the first steamboats on the river."

He paused. "The **keelboats** were popular before the steamboats came. I floated a keelboat **downstream** nearly 2,000 miles from Pittsburgh to New Orleans one time. There was no engine, so I had to haul it up the river again for the next trip. You'd **pole** through the shallows and **bushwhack** to help you along. By the time we got to **Natchez** my hands were raw and bleeding."

"Ah," murmured Marjorie, looking around the crowded living room. There were no portraits, no

---

People and Terms to Know

keelboats—long, slim boats without engines that were used for freight.
downstream—in the direction of the river's current.
pole—use a long pole to move a boat by pushing off the river bottom.
bushwhack—propel a boat by grabbing tree branches along the shore and pulling.
Natchez—Mississippi River port north of New Orleans.

▲

Flatboatmen use big sweep oars to guide their craft down the
Tennessee River.

womanly keepsakes, only a beautiful ship's bell in
the corner. It seemed that Constance lived on only
in the captain's memory.

"Then there were the **flatboats**." Captain
Snellings spoke as if he were in a daydream.
"Families built them out of wood scraps and used
them to float downstream. When they found a
likely spot, they'd turn the boat into a house, a
church, or a school. Yes, sir!" He chuckled.

Marjorie still had not heard the answer she wanted. "But what about Constance?"

The old man's face softened. "Yes. *Constance.* You know, the steamboats were a sight better than the keelboats and flatboats. Their engine power could push them **upstream** as well as down. Travelers hopped on steamboats just like they'd take a train today. I crewed on a few vessels, but I dreamed of being a captain."

Marjorie couldn't help thinking of her soldier, Jared, and his hope of becoming an officer. With great effort she turned her attention back to Captain Snellings.

"Down at the Cincinnati harbor I first laid eyes on my little *Constance,*" he was saying. "She was a beauty! Though she was a bit broad in the beam."

Marjorie was mildly shocked. "Broad in the beam" was no way to speak of your lady friend. But perhaps, she thought, manners were different out here.

"We carried lumber to Portsmouth and flour to Louisville," Captain Snellings said proudly. "We brought hogs to Memphis and cider to Vicksburg. My *Constance* was strong!" Marjorie

People and Terms to Know

upstream—against the river's current.

hoped Constance did not have to do all the heavy lifting by herself. My goodness, she thought, perhaps it was the strain from lifting that had led to her death.

"The river ran with foam."

"Now, we steamboat captains, we liked to brag," said the old man. "We said we were half alligator and half snappin' turtle, had the teeth of a coyote and the claws of a cougar. We were *tough*. So when Captain Chester challenged us to race him that day in '27, I accepted."

"Did she—fall overboard?" Marjorie scarcely dared to ask.

"Eh?" Captain Snellings frowned. "We were near **Paducah**. We'd race for five miles, Chester said, so we were off." The captain's voice took on a singsong quality. "We brought the engines to full power. We were going twelve miles an hour. We threw more fuel into the **boiler**. Black smoke poured from the chimneys. Steam shot from the pipes. The river ran with foam."

"Did Constance enjoy herself?" Marjorie asked, trying to picture the scene.

People and Terms to Know

Paducah—Ohio River port in western Kentucky.
boiler—engine on a steamboat.

"Not at first," the captain replied. "We fell behind. I had the crew cut a few wooden supports and toss them overboard. We had to make the boat lighter so we could travel faster. But at the four-mile mark the *New Albany* was still ahead of us. So I threw a cask of bacon into the boiler."

"Bacon?" Marjorie opened her mouth in surprise.

"Why, it amounted to extra fuel," Captain Snellings explained. "We leaped ahead with half a mile to go. I shook my fist at Captain Chester. 'Take *that*, you no-account flatboat mechanic!' I yelled. 'Get yourself a *real* boat next time you come a-tangling with us!'"

"And what did Constance say?" Marjorie asked, imagining a black-haired beauty on the deck alongside her handsome young husband.

"*Constance*?" Captain Snellings looked puzzled. "Why, she didn't say nothing. So I threw in another cask of bacon, and rang the bell at the front, to celebrate the victory a little early. But I'd pushed that boat past what she could take. There was a hiss, and a boom, and the next thing I knew I was in the water, and—"

Captain Snellings swallowed hard. "And what used to be *Constance* was scattered over the Ohio River all around me."

Marjorie shut her eyes tight at this horror.

"I never found another so beautiful," murmured the captain. Tears glistened in his eyes. "There's none like my *Constance*. All that's left is her bell—" He gestured to the corner.

Marjorie shut her eyes tight at this horror.

It was a bell from the steamboat, thought Marjorie. What a lovely way to remember a beautiful young wife, dead before her time. If Charles, Jared, or Thomas died, she would want something similar from them. Walking to the corner, she ran her finger along the bell's surface. The name CONSTANCE was carved on it in large capital letters.

Such a *sweet* man, she thought, to have engraved his wife's name into the bell after she had been—well, blown to bits.

It was such a *sad* tale.

And yet, sighed Marjorie, how *very* romantic!

QUESTIONS TO CONSIDER

1. Who or what was Captain Snellings talking about when he spoke of *Constance*? How do you know?

2. What does the story tell you about early steamboat captains?

3. How were steamboats different from the boats that had been in use before them?

4. How did people use rivers in early American society?

Riverboats opened up new avenues of exploration for young men seeking their fortune. One such young man describes his adventures in Mark Twain's *Life on the Mississippi*:

When we presently got under way and went poking down the broad Ohio, I became a new being, and the subject of my own admiration. I was a traveller! A word never had tasted so good in my mouth before. I had an exultant sense of being bound for mysterious lands and distant climes which I never have felt in so uplifting a degree since. I was in such a glorified condition that all ignoble feelings departed out of me, and I was able to look down and pity the untravelled with a compassion that had hardly a trace of contempt in it. Still, when we stopped at villages and wood-yards, I could not help lolling carelessly upon the railings of the boiler deck to enjoy the envy of the country boys on the bank. If they did not seem to discover me, I presently sneezed to attract their attention, or moved to a position where they could not help seeing me. And as soon as I knew they saw me I gaped and stretched, and gave other signs of being mightily bored with travelling.

*   *   *

I kept my hat off all the time, and stayed where the wind and the sun could strike me, because I wanted to get the bronzed and weather-beaten look of an old traveller. Before the second day was half gone, I experienced a joy which filled me with the purest gratitude; for I saw that the skin had begun to blister and peel off my face and neck. I wished that the boys and girls at home could see me now.

The Trail of Tears

BY DIANE WILDE

Etowah was seventeen years old when white men from the U.S. government told his people that they must leave their home and move to new lands in the West. The **Cherokee** loved the land where they had lived for many generations. They had worked hard to care for and improve their land. By the time Etowah was born, most families were living in log cabins on small farms. They did not want to move.

The Cherokee had been trading with white settlers for more than 100 years. But after the Revolutionary War ended, many settlers wanted the rich lands

---

People and Terms to Know

Cherokee—Native American group originally living in the land that now covers parts of the states of Georgia, Alabama, Kentucky, South Carolina, North Carolina, and Tennessee.

Thousands of Cherokee died of hunger, cold, and disease on the Trail

where Etowah's people lived. Greedy settlers destroyed many villages and took over Cherokee land. Fighting broke out. Indians killed settlers, and settlers killed Indians. The U. S. government did little. But, in 1830, **President Andrew Jackson** got Congress to pass the **Indian Removal Act**.

Fighting broke out. Indians killed settlers, and settlers killed Indians.

Now, in May of 1838, Federal troops had come to round up the remaining Cherokee tribes. The soldiers gave people only a short time to gather a few belongings from their homes.

Etowah was shocked. He hadn't thought it would come to this. He hurried to grab his special leather-bound book. It had clean white pages to write on. Uncle William had given it to him, along with a beautiful quill pen and a bottle of ink. Etowah had used the book to practice writing the Cherokee alphabet, created by the great and honored Cherokee scholar, **Sequoyah**.

People and Terms to Know

President Andrew Jackson—(1767–1845) seventh president of the United States. He served from 1829 to 1837.

Indian Removal Act—bill that allowed Federal troops to remove large numbers of Indians from their traditional lands and resettle them in lands farther west.

Sequoyah (sih•KWOY•uh)—(c. 1770–1843) Cherokee leader who created a new alphabet, which he called "talking leaves," so that Cherokee could read and write their own language.

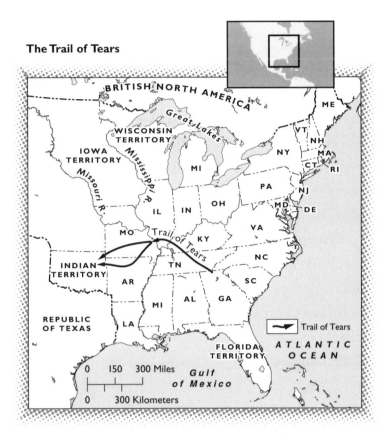

The Trail of Tears

Now Etowah decided to use the book to keep a record of the journey they would be taking. He also took the pen and ink, his knife, and the coat with big pockets. There wasn't enough time to gather very many things, so people had to leave many valuable belongings behind.

Many of the soldiers were mean and rough as they led Etowah and his family to the stockades.

There they were locked up with others from their village to wait until they could begin the journey west.

The soldiers separated Etowah, his father, and his older brother from Etowah's mother and sister. Even some very small children were taken from their mothers. Then the soldiers took the men and women to different stockades. The tears started to flow that very first day.

Three days later, Etowah began to write in his book. He found a small, hidden corner in the stockade where he could write in private. Sometimes he wrote in Cherokee and sometimes in English. Like many of his people, he could read and write in both languages.

Month of the Planting Moon (May)

My people are very unhappy now. We have been moved to a large stockade and are not allowed to leave it. Most of the soldiers treat us badly and show no respect, though two of them seem worried about us. They try to help us by bringing us fresh water and more blankets.

Father feels much anger in his heart. The soldiers do not give us enough food, and we are not allowed to go out to hunt for ourselves. We have had no contact with my mother or sister since we came here. We hope they are treated better than we are, but I can hear many women and girls crying during the night. I feel very angry today.

*　*　*

Month of the Green Corn Moon (June)

Yesterday, the first group of travelers left the camp. Federal guards took them away by boat. The soldiers took some of us to the river shore to help load supplies. The boats were not large enough for so many, and the people were very crowded.

People say that the trip takes almost three moons.

I saw my mother and sister among the passengers and quickly said goodbye. I am angry and sad that they are made to go without father and I. People say that the trip takes almost three moons. I do not think that the supplies we loaded will be enough to get so many people through to the end of their journey. I wonder if my family will ever be together again.

*　*　*

Month of the Ripe Corn Moon (July)

We have been living in this place for almost two full circles of the moon. It has not rained during all this time and the days are very hot. There is little shade to protect us from the burning sun.

Many people grow sick from the heat and the bad food. Some people have already died—mostly older people and small children. The crying I hear at night is closer now because now the men are also weeping.

Our Chief, **John Ross**, has asked the U. S. government if we who remain may be allowed to stay here until the weather is cooler. It is strange to me that the white man's government is so mean to men like Chief Ross. Like many of our people, he has more white blood than Cherokee.

* * *

Month of the End of the Fruit Moon (August)

I have been very sad for many days. Last week Uncle Stephen died from fever. He was Uncle William's older brother. Uncle William made the leather cover for the book I write in. When the soldiers came to lock us up, Uncle William was hiding in the mountains with his family. I don't think they have been able to find him. I am glad that he left so early and was able to spare himself and his family from what happened to us.

People and Terms to Know

John Ross—(1790–1866) most important Cherokee chief at the time of forced removal to Indian Territory. He was chief of the united Cherokee nation until he died.

* * *

Month of the Nut Moon (September)

Chief John Ross told us that we will leave today to go west with the last of his three groups.

People were busy this morning getting ready for the journey, but their voices were silent and their faces looked sad. We are all sad and angry most of the time now. Though many are sick, they worked hard today, loading wagons and preparing horses, oxen, and mules. Chief Ross decided to go with his family by boat. They waved to us as they set off.

> *We are all sad and angry most of the time now.*

* * *

Month of the Harvest Moon (October)

Word reached us yesterday that the last group left the camps at the beginning of this month. They are traveling overland behind us. The nights are getting colder, and we don't have enough blankets. Unless we get more supplies, I don't see how we will be able to survive the colder winter to come.

* * *

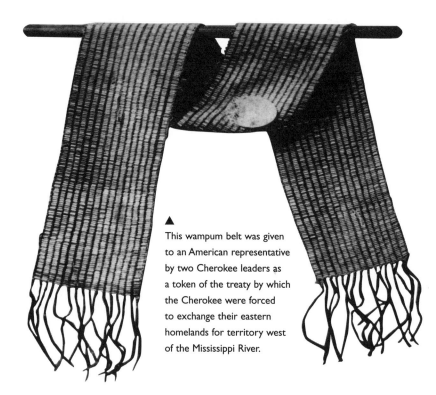

▲
This wampum belt was given to an American representative by two Cherokee leaders as a token of the treaty by which the Cherokee were forced to exchange their eastern homelands for territory west of the Mississippi River.

Month of the Trading Moon (November)

We had sleet, snow, and freezing temperatures yesterday morning and saw dangerous <u>ice floes</u> on the Mississippi River. I do not feel strong enough to write as much in these shorter, darker days. The air is so cold now that I have to thaw my ink over a fire before I can dip the pen into it. Since we often don't have enough wood for a fire, I cannot write as often as I would like.

People and Terms to Know

ice floes—large, floating fragments of sheet ice.

Month of the Windy Moon (March)

We finally arrived at our new home yesterday. We were among the last of our parties to reach this strange, new place. It is dry and flat here, and there are almost no trees at all. I miss the forests of home. I don't know how we are going to farm this dry land. The hard winter weather has lasted until now. On just one night during our journey, twenty-two people died from the extreme cold.

* * *

As many as 14,000 to 17,000 people began the terrible journey from southeastern Tennessee and northwestern Georgia to the Indian Territories of northeastern Oklahoma. This journey became known as "The Trail of Tears." It was a distance of about 800 miles, and more than 4,000 people died, or about one-fourth of the total number. The journey, which the government thought would take about 80 days, actually took about 140 to 160 days. About 1,500 people died in the camps before starting and another 1,600 died during the journey. More than 800 were so weak from the journey that they died after arriving in Oklahoma. Like Etowah's

Uncle William, several hundred Cherokee stayed in the distant parts of the old tribal lands in the hills of North Carolina.

QUESTIONS TO CONSIDER

1. Why were the Cherokee tribes forced to leave their lands?

2. What are some examples of why this journey was called "The Trail of Tears"?

3. How would you describe the planning that the government put into moving the Cherokee people to their new land in the West?

4. What challenges did the Cherokee face in their new land?

Soft Rain: A Story of the Cherokee Trail of Tears
by Cornelia Cornelissen

In 1838, Soft Rain, a nine-year-old Cherokee, and her family are forced to relocate their home after the U.S. government takes away their land. The terrible human tragedies that resulted from the Cherokee's forced relocation hit home in this moving fictional story.

Cherokee Sister
by Debbie Dadey

Debbie Dadey presents an unusual story in which a Cherokee girl and her family share a friendly relationship with local whites before the tragic events of the Indian Removal Act begin to unfold.

On the Long Way Home
by Elisabeth Stewart

Elisabeth Stewart's story is based on her own great-grandmother's experience of escaping from white soldiers who are marching her captive people along The Trail of Tears. After escaping, the young girl, Meli, and her older brother make their way back to their home in the Appalachian Mountains.

The West

Lewis and Clark Meet the Shoshone

BY JUDITH LLOYD YERO

In 1803, the **Louisiana Purchase** expanded the western border of the United States from the Mississippi River to the Rocky Mountains. No one knew what challenges this vast territory held. Could the land be farmed? What resources might be found—animals, plants, water? What were the best routes to the West? Was trade with the Indians possible? Before America's population could safely expand, more information was needed.

People and Terms to Know

Louisiana Purchase—(1803) agreement by which the United States bought the western half of the Mississippi River basin from France for less than three cents per acre. The purchase doubled the size of the United States.

The Shoshone woman Sacagawea guides the explorers Lewis (center left) and

President Thomas Jefferson asked his secretary, **Captain Meriwether Lewis**, to lead an **expedition**— called the **Corps of Discovery**—through the unex-plored territory. As his co-leader, Lewis chose **Captain William Clark**. Clark's first job was to find skilled people, such as carpenters and black-smiths, to be part of the expedition. He also found interpreters to help the team talk to the Indians they would meet along the way. Lewis's job was to record information about the trip. Lewis stud-ied a number of sciences to prepare for this job. He wanted to be able to describe accurately the

He wanted to be able to describe accurately the geography, animals, and natural history of the land for future travelers.

People and Terms to Know

Captain Meriwether Lewis—(1774–1809) leader of the first team of explorers to travel to the Pacific Northwest (1804–1806). To prepare for the trip, Lewis studied botany, zoology, and navigation. The information he recorded was valuable to settlers who planned to move westward.

expedition—journey taken for exploration or battle.

Corps of Discovery—(1804–1806) also called the Lewis and Clark Expedition. First U.S. overland expedition to the Pacific coast and back to explore the territories that were part of the Louisiana Purchase.

Captain William Clark—(1770–1838) American frontiersman who shared leadership of the expedition to the Pacific Northwest with Meriwether Lewis. Clark rescued the expedition from disaster on several occasions. He was the mapmaker and artist of the expedition. He was later involved in the development of the Missouri Territory.

geography, animals, and natural history of the land for future travelers.

On May 14, 1804, the Lewis and Clark Expedition began the long row up the Missouri River. The group was made up of about forty-five men and Lewis's dog, Seaman. On November 2, they camped for the winter near the **Mandan** tribe of North Dakota.

A French Canadian named Charbonneau was living with the Mandans. Charbonneau's wife was a young **Shoshone** girl of about sixteen named **Sacagawea**. At age ten, she had been kidnapped by another tribe, but she still spoke the Shoshone language.

Lewis and Clark knew they would need to buy horses from the Shoshone in order to cross the

---

People and Terms to Know

Mandan—American Plains Indians who spoke the Sioux language. The Mandans were a peaceful people who hunted buffalo and farmed. They lived in the Missouri River Valley near present-day Bismarck, North Dakota.

Shoshone (shoh•SHOH•nee)—(also spelled Shoshoni) North American Indian group that occupied the territory from southeastern California across Nevada and northwestern Utah into southern Idaho and western Wyoming. The Northern Shoshone had horses from as early as 1680.

Sacagawea (sah•kah•juh•WAY•ah)—(c. 1786–1812) Shoshone woman who, carrying her infant son on her back, traveled thousands of wilderness miles with the Lewis and Clark Expedition. She acted as translator for the group with the Shoshone and provided the expedition with edible fruits and vegetables. Sacagawea means "Bird Woman."

mountains. Sacagawea was just the person they needed to speak with the Shoshone. So they agreed to hire Charbonneau, if he would bring along his wife. When the Expedition left the Mandans in April of 1805, Sacagawea and her infant son went with them.

Here are shortened versions of some of the journal entries kept by the men of the Expedition.

April 7, 1805

We left **Fort Mandan**. Thirty-one men, the Indian woman Sacagawea, and her baby went up the river. The woman and child will show the Indians that we are a peaceful group.

April 9, 1805

The Indian woman found a nice supply of wild artichokes that the mice buried. They'll make a nice treat with the beaver we caught. I particularly like the tail and liver.

People and Terms to Know

Fort Mandan—fort built by the Lewis and Clark Expedition near the Mandan camp; it was completed November 20, 1804. This is where the expedition spent the winter of 1804–1805. The fort had eight connected log cabins arranged to form a V shape, with a fence at the open end.

April 20, 1805

The wind rose again and blew so hard that the canoes took in a great deal of water and nearly sank. The sand blew off the sand bars and beaches so that we could hardly see. It was like a thick fog. It took us about two hours to travel about two and a half miles. We had high wind and snow this day.

April 24, 1805

Sore eyes are a common problem among the party. The wind sometimes blows the sand into such clouds that you are unable to see the opposite bank of the river. The sand is in everything. We must eat, drink, and breathe it.

The wind sometimes blows the sand into such clouds that you are unable to see the opposite bank of the river.

May 14, 1805

Charbonneau can't swim and is scared of water. When a big wind hit the boat, he started crying to God for mercy. By the time he got the boat righted, it was full of water. All our maps and papers floated out of the boat. Sacagawea, who was sitting in the back of the boat, just reached out nice as you please and caught everything as it was floating by. She's sure got a lot more spunk than that husband of hers.

◀ William Clark

July 27, 1805

We expected to meet the Shoshone here at the Three Forks of the Missouri, but they may be farther up the river. Or they may have gone over the mountains to the Columbia River to fish. Three Forks is where Sacagawea was kidnapped by the **Minitari**. Nothing seems to bother her. If she has enough to eat and a few trinkets to wear, I believe she would be perfectly content anywhere.

People and Terms to Know

Minitari—(also called Hidatsa and Gros Ventres of the Missouri) American Plains Indian people of Sioux descent who lived on the upper Missouri River. They farmed and hunted bison and other large game on the grasslands.

Meriwether Lewis ▶

August 5, 1805

Passed over rapids worse than ever. It is very hard, and we get very tired trying to pass through them. Sometimes we must row straight up for 3 or 4 feet in a short distance. . . .

August 8, 1805

Sacagawea's people call this high rock "the beaver's head." She says we're not far from their summer home. Capt. Lewis has decided to take a few men and go off to find the Shoshone.

August 11, 1805

After marching for about five miles, we saw an Indian on horseback coming towards us. He was

Shoshone. Capt. Lewis spread his blanket on the ground as a sign of friendship—an invitation to talk. The Shoshone called us "tab-ba-bone," which means "white man" in their language. I even rolled up my shirt sleeve to let him see the color of my skin, but seeing several of us approaching must have frightened him. He suddenly turned his horse about, leaped the creek, and disappeared.

August 13, 1805

We saw more natives today. Many of them ran. We approached an elderly woman who held her head down as if she expected to die. Capt. Lewis took the old woman's hand and showed her his skin. He painted her cheeks with some red dye, which Sacagawea said was a sign of peace. The woman led us to about 60 warriors mounted on excellent horses, riding at full speed in our direction. The natives who fled must have told them about us. The men dismounted from their horses and hugged us in their way, placing their left cheek to ours and yelling the word *ah-hi-e*. It means "I am much pleased." We were all smeared with their grease and paint till I was heartily tired of the national hug.

The natives sat in a circle around us and pulled off their **moccasins** before they would smoke the pipe. They do this to show that they would go barefoot if they are not sincere. Using the common sign language, Capt. Lewis gave their chief, Cameahwait, the flag and told him it was a symbol of peace among white men. All the women and children of the camp gathered around to look at us. We were the first white persons they had ever seen.

August 15, 1805

Capt. Lewis told the Shoshone we had an Indian woman and her baby with us—a woman who had been taken from their people. He convinced the chief to come with us to where we would meet Capt. Clark and the rest of the party. Some Indians thought they were walking into an **ambush**, but the chief finally agreed to come.

August 16, 1805

One of the men killed a deer today, and I have never seen people eat as the Indians do. They were starved and devoured nearly the whole animal without cooking it.

People and Terms to Know

moccasins—soft leather slippers worn by American Indians.
ambush—surprise attack by people who are hidden.

August 17, 1805

Capt. Clark arrived with Charbonneau and Sacagawea. She danced ahead, sucking her fingers to show that these were her people. Their meeting was really happy, especially between Sacagawea and an Indian woman who had been taken prisoner with her but later escaped.

Everything we had surprised them.

When Sacagawea saw the chief, she covered his head with her blanket. He was her brother! She finally stopped crying long enough to interpret for us. Everything we had surprised them. The Shoshone were fascinated by our canoes and Captain Lewis's black servant, York. They eyed the Captain's dog, Seaman, hungrily. They called Capt. Lewis's air-gun "great medicine." We learned that to keep the Shoshone in good spirits, you shouldn't carry on too much business at one time.

These half-starved people were living on berries and roots they gathered on the plains, but they were generous with what little they had. They had only a few weapons and used a sharpened elk horn to cut their wood. We gave the chief some dried squash, which we'd brought from the Mandans. He boiled them and said they were the best thing he had ever tasted except the small lump of sugar Sacagawea had given him. The Captain told him that the white men could help his nation live in the country below the mountains where they might grow corn, beans, and squashes. He appeared much pleased with what the Captain said.

*   *   *

On August 31, 1805, the Corps of Discovery left Shoshone land with 29 horses and one mule. The animals had cost less than 100 dollars in goods— shirts, leggings, a few knives and axes, and other articles that the Shoshone prized.

Sacagawea and her son went with the Expedition to the Pacific Ocean and, in 1806, back to the land of the Mandan. She did not act as a guide, as some stories would suggest, but the men of the expedition respected her courage and strength. There is no known picture of Sacagawea, but her image is often seen in statues, paintings, and on the U. S. dollar coin.

QUESTIONS TO CONSIDER

1. What kind of information about the Louisiana Territory did Thomas Jefferson want the Lewis and Clark Expedition to gather?

2. How do you think later travelers in the Northwest Territory benefited from the information gathered by the Expedition?

3. Why was it so important for the Expedition to find the Shoshone?

4. What were some of the problems the Expedition encountered?

Jim Beckwourth Lives with the Crow

BY DANNY MILLER

The day my dead brother returned to us was the happiest day our village had ever seen. My mother fell to the ground and kissed the earth in thanks. My father raised his arms to the Great Spirit. My brothers and sisters sang songs of joy.

Among the hundreds of people who welcomed the long-lost member of our tribe, I was the only one who would ever know the truth. The man who returned to us on that day was not my brother. He was not even a member of our tribe. He was a black mountain man named **Jim Beckwourth**.

People and Terms to Know

Jim Beckwourth—(1798–1866) African-American frontiersman, trapper, and adventurer.

A Crow woman carries firewood to her tipi.

My name is Running Deer, and I am a **Crow** Indian. We call ourselves **Absaroka**. In your way of measuring time, it is the year 1834. The strange story of my non-Indian brother began almost six winters ago.

One day, some of our **braves** returned from a hunt with a wild tale. They had met two **trappers** who had wandered into Crow territory. One of them, a white man named Caleb Greenwood, spoke our language. He told the braves that the other trapper was born Crow! He said that his friend had been kidnapped as a child during one of the bloody attacks on our people by the **Cheyenne**. Later, Greenwood explained, the boy was bought by white people and raised in a distant place.

News of the returned Crow spread like wildfire through our village. We all remembered the stories of that horrible day. During that attack, my older

---

People and Terms to Know

Crow—American Indian people who lived in the region between the Platte and Yellowstone Rivers.

Absaroka—name that the Crow used for their people and their land.

braves—North American Indian warriors.

trappers—people whose occupation is trapping animals, such as beavers, and selling their pelts, or furs.

Cheyenne—group of Algonquin-speaking North American Indians.

brother had been ripped from my mother's arms. The pain of that loss was like a deep scar on our family's spirit. "Could it be my son?" wailed my mother when she heard the story about the trapper.

During that attack, my older brother had been ripped from my mother's arms.

With the blessing of my father, Chief Big Bowl, a party of braves set out to capture the mysterious stranger. When they returned, everyone in the village lined up in two rows. They were wearing their best clothes to welcome the trapper.

None of us had ever seen a man like this before. He had dark skin, gold chains around his neck, several earrings in each ear, and long braided hair tied back with colorful ribbons. I couldn't believe that this tall, strange man might be my blood brother.

One by one, members of our tribe walked up to the man and looked at him closely. Some came right up to his face. Children poked at his chest. Old women bent down to look at his feet. Finally, my gray-haired mother came up with my father. A hush fell over the crowd when my mother reached up and touched the man's face. She closed her eyes, thinking of that dreaded day when the Cheyenne had carried off her baby boy. Then she remembered something that could settle the question of the stranger's identity.

"If this is my son," my mother said slowly, "he will have a mole on one of his eyes."

At once a swarm of women's hands reached over and started pulling on the poor man's eyelids, stretching them as far as they could go. A quick yelp came from my mother when she spotted it. Sure enough, there on the man's left eyelid was a small brown mole.

"My son! You are really my son!" my mother shrieked.

"The dead is alive again," shouted my father, giving his newfound son a big hug. "The lost one is found!"

An enormous noise went up in our village. I heard later that nearby tribes worried we were on the attack. My father named the trapper Morning Star. My four sisters hugged the brother they had never known. They quickly removed his clothes and dressed him in the finest, most beautiful beadwork, leggings, and moccasins our people could offer.

Morning Star looked pleased to be with our family. Through an interpreter, he told us stories of how, in his recent travels, he had killed hundreds of **Blackfoot**, our mortal enemies.

My father asked Morning Star if he wanted to take one of the young girls in our village as a bride.

I did not see my ancestors reflected in his eyes.

All three of Chief Black Lodge's pretty daughters were brought forward: Stillwater, Black Fish, and Three Roads. Morning Star chose Stillwater, a friendly girl who seemed delighted to have her future so suddenly changed.

My mother and sisters raised a **tipi** for Morning Star and his bride. They filled it with soft hides, furs, and cooking pots brimming with food.

Galloping Pony, my older brother, gave the newlyweds a gift of twenty fine horses. I gave the couple a bow, a beaded **quiver** filled with arrows, and a war shield made from tough buffalo hide. My new brother smiled at me. Something was very different about his face. I did not see my ancestors reflected in his eyes.

People and Terms to Know

Blackfoot—Native American people of Montana and southwest Canada.

tipi—cone-shaped Indian shelter made by stretching animal skins over poles.

quiver—portable case for arrows.

▲

A Crow woman uses a scraper made of elk antler to remove the hair from an animal hide.

A few days later, Morning Star joined us in a small war party. During a struggle, we found our new brother in hand-to-hand combat with a fierce Blackfoot warrior. Morning Star was victorious! In the end, we returned to our village with eleven **scalps**. Morning Star had drawn the first blood from our enemy. He was a hero!

I admired my brother but still had doubts about who he was. The next day, after feasting on a fat **buffalo**, Morning Star and I wandered off to a

People and Terms to Know

scalps—skins covering the top of the head, cut away from an enemy as a battle trophy.

buffalo—oxlike mammal, staple of the Plains Indians' diet.

nearby creek. He was now learning our language. When I asked him questions about himself, he told me the truth.

I was right! He was not Crow after all—that was just a joke his friend Caleb Greenwood had made up. His real name was Jim Beckwourth. He said that a long time ago his mother's people had come from a distant land across the sea called Africa. His mother was a slave to the white people, and his father was her master. He was born in a place called Virginia but moved to St. Louis when he was a boy. From there he had escaped and made his way to the frontier, where he became a trapper.

Now it was too late to tell the truth.

Jim told me that he hadn't planned to lie to our people. He just thought he should go along with us when he was captured or he might be in danger. He also hoped to trap beavers in our streams. Now it was too late to tell the truth. No one would believe him. Besides, he really loved us as if we were his family. I liked the stranger. I decided to keep his secret and let my parents believe that their long-lost son had returned.

Beckwourth led our people in many victories. He became one of our most respected war chiefs.

My father gave Jim a new name after each big victory. He was called Bull's Robe, Medicine Calf, and Bloody Arm.

Since the season of Falling Leaves began, I've noticed that my brother seems troubled. Yesterday Jim told me that it is time for him to go. He said he needs to see his own people again. He never thought he would stay with us this long. "I only visited the Indian territory to satisfy my thirst for adventure," he explained.

Today Jim spoke to our village. "I am going to leave you for a few moons," he said, "to visit my friends among the white men." He promised he would return by the season of Green Grass. He urged us to remember everything he taught us. My mother and father are sad, but they are sure their son will return.

The man named Jim Beckwourth brought much joy to our people. Although he was not born Crow, he became one through his deeds. I will miss my brother, but I know he is moving on to his next adventure. I do not think we will see Jim Beckwourth again.

◀ Jim Beckwourth

*　*　*

Mountain Men of the Old West

Mountain men like Jim Beckwourth played an important role in developing the West during the early 1800s. They led rough, lonely lives as they roamed the wild frontier. Although these men loved adventure, they also came to the wilderness to make money. They made their living as fur trappers, hunting beavers for their valuable fur. Mountain men also led expeditions to wild areas. They had a lot of experience in dealing directly with Native American tribes. Most mountain men could speak several Indian languages. This made them valuable to the federal government and other groups that were moving to the frontier. Some mountain men even acted as Indian agents and worked to settle conflicts between the government and the tribes. In addition to Beckwourth, some of the other famous mountain men included Kit Carson, Jim Bridger, Joe Walker, and Jedediah Smith.

QUESTIONS TO CONSIDER

1. Why did the Crow think that Jim Beckwourth was one of them?

2. How did Beckwourth adapt to life among the Crow Indians?

3. Why did Beckwourth deceive the Crow about his real identity?

4. What skills did mountain men like Beckwourth have?

5. How were mountain men important to the exploration and development of the West?

The Texas Revolution Begins

BY JANE LEDER

Back in 1823, the area we now call Texas was part of Mexico. Americans like me were looking for a new beginning, so when my wife and I heard that **Stephen F. Austin** was starting a colony in Mexico, we decided to go there. It would be the adventure of our lives.

It was Austin's father, Moses, who took the first steps toward building this American colony. Moses died before finishing his plans, so Stephen followed through with them. In 1821, he received approval to settle 300 American families on 200,000 acres.

By the time my family and I arrived, Austin was in charge. He set up a system of laws and made

---

People and Terms to Know

Stephen F. Austin—(1793–1836) man considered the founder of the state of Texas.

Mexican forces under Antonio López de Santa Anna overwhelm Texas defenders of the Alamo on March 6, 1836.

plans for roads, schools, sawmills and **granaries**. I admired his skills and positive attitude.

Our colony wasn't much at the start. We were only about a dozen families. We built log cabins with no windows and no floors. The cabins were close together to give us protection from the Indians. A tribe called the **Karankawa** could make life hard for us. They would steal our horses and anything else they could find. But, at that time, there was no fighting between us.

Over the next couple of years, the colony did well. More and more settlers arrived to start new colonies. But we had some problems with the Mexican government. They charged us a heavy fee whenever we tried to sell our goods in Mexico. There were no public schools, as they had promised. They would not allow us to have black slaves to work in our fields, and we were not allowed to pray the way we wanted.

Then, in 1830, the Mexican government passed a new law. It said no new settlers could come to

People and Terms to Know

granaries—buildings for storing grain.
Karankawa—term that includes several Native American groups that lived near the Austin colony in Texas.

Texas. The government no longer favored our colonies. Mexico's agreements with Austin and other colonizers had called for only Roman Catholic colonists. The government said most of us were only pretending to be Roman Catholic. (I must admit that was true.) The government also said we were not trying to fit in with our Mexican neighbors, since we spoke only English. Finally, the government did not want us to have slaves.

By now, more Americans lived in Texas than Mexicans.

By now, more Americans lived in Texas than Mexicans. I guess the government was worried that we would revolt and take over, so they sent more soldiers to Texas.

In 1832, Texans called a meeting. The **Convention of 1832** met in San Felipe, Mexico. Sixteen Texas settlements sent representatives to the Convention. They wrote a petition asking Mexico to repeal the 1830 law. They also asked to form a separate state of Texas within the Mexican Republic.

People and Terms to Know

Convention of 1832—meeting that took place in San Felipe, Mexico. Fifty-eight delegates from 16 Texas settlements met and wrote a petition to the Mexican government. Officials of Mexico declared the convention illegal.

Austin urged the colonists to remain loyal to Mexico. But they insisted, and, against his better judgment, Austin took the petition to the Mexican government. He met with President **Antonio López de Santa Anna**.

Santa Anna refused to grant the request for statehood. Then he had Austin put in prison because he thought Austin might be planning a revolution. Austin was kept in prison for 18 months until July 1835.

Santa Anna set out to crush rebellions in Texas. In October of 1835, he sent a force of about 100 Mexicans to **Gonzales**. They had orders to take back a cannon that had been given to the settlers for defense against the Indians. The cannon was practically useless anyway. It had no ammunition. But the Texans cut bars of iron and loaded the cannon. They also took a piece of white cotton about six feet long and made a flag. Someone painted a picture of

People and Terms to Know

Antonio López de Santa Anna—(1794–1876) president of Mexico who led the Mexican forces against the Texans. He was captured at the Battle of San Jacinto but was allowed to return to Mexico.

Gonzales—settlement in Texas located where the Guadalupe and San Marcos Rivers meet.

the old cannon in the middle with a lone star above it. Underneath were the words, "Come and take it."

The Texans hung the flag on the cannon, aimed at the Mexicans, and fired the shot that started the **Texas Revolution**. The Texans' only arms were **Bowie knives** and long rifles. They had no swords or pistols. Yet after a short fight, the Mexicans retreated. They lost one soldier. We had no losses—only a minor gunshot wound and one bloody nose.

His plan was to keep retreating in order to wear down the Mexican troops.

At the start of the Texas Revolution, **Sam Houston** became commander of the Texas Army. He knew that there were many more Mexican troops than Texas troops. But he had a plan. His plan was to keep retreating in order to wear down the Mexican troops. Meanwhile, Austin went to the United States to try to get more support.

People and Terms to Know

Texas Revolution—(1835–1836) war that began with the Battle of Gonzales and ended in victory for the Texans at the Battle of San Jacinto.

Bowie knives—long knives made famous by Jim Bowie (c. 1796–1836). Bowie was a frontiersman who moved to Texas in 1828 and joined the fight for independence from Mexico. He commanded the volunteer forces at the Alamo and died there.

Sam Houston—(1793–1863) commander-in-chief of the armies of Texas, whose forces defeated the Mexicans at the Battle of San Jacinto. Houston was elected the first president of the Republic of Texas in 1836. Later, he served as senator from Texas and as the governor of Texas.

Jim Bowie led the fight at the **Battle of Concepción**. As we heard it later from our friend **Noah Smithwick**, the Mexicans opened up fire with a cannon. Our men lay low, and the ammunition crashed through the pecan trees overhead. A lot of pecans were shot off the trees. Some of the men picked the nuts up and ate them.

Bowie kept yelling, "Keep under cover, boys, and reserve your fire. We haven't a man to spare." If he had been obeyed, we wouldn't have lost anyone. But war does funny things to men. They sometimes get too excited, too eager. A man named Dick Andrews just couldn't wait for orders. He paid the price. Smithwick found him lying on the ground, with blood gushing from a hole in his left side.

"Dick," Smithwick cried. "Are you hurt?"

"Yes, Smith," he replied. "I'm killed. Lay me down."

We lost Andrews but won the battle. However, the war wasn't over by a long shot.

People and Terms to Know

Battle of Concepción—battle that took place on October 28, 1835, in which Jim Bowie and 90 Texans defeated 450 Mexicans near San Antonio, Texas.

Noah Smithwick—(1808–1899) early Texas pioneer. He wrote a book called *The Evolution of a State* (1900). In the book, he paints a clear picture of what life was like at that exciting time in Texas history.

*   *   *

On January 17, 1836, Sam Houston sent Colonel
Jim Bowie and 25 men to San Antonio. They had
orders to destroy the fort called the
Alamo. Then they were to move
east with the cannons. But Bowie
didn't have horses or mules to
move the cannons. He decided
that it would be better to stay there
and hold his position.

*He wanted
to end the
revolution once
and for all.*

B y February 9, more troops had arrived at the
Alamo. These included 130 cavalry under Colonel
William Travis, **Davy Crockett**, and 14 Tennessee
Mounted Volunteers. About February 23, 1836, the
Mexican army arrived in San Antonio. Santa Anna
led the troops himself. He was determined to win
this key location after losing San Antonio in an
earlier battle. He wanted to end the revolution
once and for all. Santa Anna ordered his men to
"take no prisoners."

People and Terms to Know

Alamo—old mission in San Antonio, Texas, where Texan heroes were massacred by Santa Anna's forces on March 6, 1836. News of Texans' bravery
in the terrible battle gave strength to the cause for Texas independence.

Davy Crockett—(1786–1836) pioneer, politician, and frontier hero. In
1836, he fought and died at the Alamo.

▲

Texans under Sam Houston surprise and defeat Mexicans under Santa Anna at the Battle of San Jacinto on April 21, 1836.

Over the next two weeks, the Mexican forces grew to more than 5,000 men. The Texans—a total of 189—defended the Alamo bravely for 13 days. But on the morning of March 6, the Mexicans stormed the mission. Bowie was **bayoneted** while lying sick in his bed. Crockett, along with six other defenders, survived the battle, but Santa Anna ordered that they be killed. Not one Texan fighter was left alive.

People and Terms to Know

bayoneted—killed by a bayonet, a dagger-like blade attached to the end of a rifle.

Sam Houston vowed to **avenge** the defenders of the Alamo. He ordered the attack that resulted in the **Battle of San Jacinto** on April 21, 1836. There the Texas Army soundly defeated the Mexicans. The battle for Texas was won! The first Congress of the independent Republic of Texas met in Austin, the frontier site selected to be the first capital. Sam Houston became its first president, and in 1845, Texas became the 28th state of the United States.

QUESTIONS TO CONSIDER

1. Why do you think people like the narrator moved to Texas?

2. What were some of the problems American settlers had with the Mexican government? What problems did the Mexican government have with them?

3. How did the colonists attempt to resolve these problems? What was the result?

4. Who were some of the major figures in the Texas Revolution?

5. What does it mean to Texans to "remember the Alamo"?

People and Terms to Know

avenge—get revenge for.
Battle of San Jacinto—battle fought on April 21, 1836, in which forces led by Sam Houston defeated the Mexican forces led by Santa Anna. This battle ended the Texas Revolution and secured Texas independence.

A Line in the Sand
by Sherry Garland

Sherry Garland tells the story of a thirteen-year-old farm girl, Lucinda Lawrence, who documents in her diary the events before and after the battles of the Texas Revolution. Lucinda's fears about seeing her father and brother go off to fight the Mexicans are movingly revealed as her family and friends are swept into war.

Boy in the Alamo
by Margaret Cousins

Margaret Cousins presents the siege of the Alamo through the eyes of twelve-year-old Billy Campbell.

Susanna of the Alamo
by John Jakes

The story of Susanna Dickinson and her infant daughter, the only survivors of the Battle of the Alamo, gives readers a firsthand viewpoint of the terrible battle as it rages around the mother and daughter.

The Oregon Trail

BY JUDITH CONAWAY

Independence, Missouri, April 29, 1848

Independence—it is a fitting name! From this place, thousands of people set out to find independent lives in the West. My family and I hope to do the same someday. In the meantime, we are building a successful business based on the wagon trains.

I arrived here in **Independence** early this morning by steamboat, after a pleasant journey from **St. Charles**. My brother, Justin, and his wife, Adela, met me at the dock.

People and Terms to Know

Independence—town in Missouri near the end of the line for steamboat transportation on the Missouri River.

St. Charles—old trading town in Missouri, just north of St. Louis, located where the Missouri, Mississippi, and Illinois Rivers meet.

A wagon train traveling along the Oregon Trail nears the Sweetwater River.

Independence is swarming with people. They all need wagons, oxen, mules, tools, supplies, and guides. We are traders and will be happy to supply their needs. This year, for the first time, our supply train will travel with the wagon train. It was Justin's idea. At first, he did not agree that Adela and I should go along, but we have changed his mind.

> *They all need wagons, oxen, mules, tools, supplies, and guides.*

Independence, May 4, 1848

This morning we visited the workshop of Mr. **Hiram Young**, who is building the wagons for our journey. Mr. Young and Justin were soon talking eagerly of the Mexican peace. The **Treaty of Guadalupe Hidalgo** has added valuable new territories to the United States and has led to the reopening of the **Santa Fe Trail**. That is very good news for our business.

People and Terms to Know

Hiram Young—freed slave who used his skills in wagon-building, wheel-making, and trading to become one of the wealthiest citizens of Independence, Missouri.

Treaty of Guadalupe Hidalgo (GWAHD•uh•LOO•pay ih•DAHL•goh)— formal agreement that ended the Mexican-American War in February 1848, and gave the territories of New Mexico, Arizona, California, Utah, and Nevada to the United States.

Santa Fe Trail—trading route between Independence, Missouri, and Santa Fe, New Mexico.

Overland Trails, 1850

Adela and I examined our wagons with great interest. We found everything as perfectly fitted out as on a ship. We were also pleased to hear that Mr. Young will be sending several repair wagons along with our train. We leave one week from today!

Independence, May 9

Our dear friend Mr. **Louis Vieux** arrived unexpectedly today. He is such a wise man! He has

---

People and Terms to Know

Louis Vieux—(1809–1872) tribal leader of the Potawatomi Indians and a businessman. He operated trading posts in various places before settling on the Vermilion River. He owned the town site of Louisville, Kansas, which bears his name. He was widely respected for his generosity, public spirit, and honesty.

---

made many trips to Washington, D.C., on behalf of the **Potawatomi** tribe. In recognition of his wise counsel, the federal government has granted him land in Kansas on the Vermilion River. We will gladly take him to his new home. I believe he plans to set up a blacksmith shop there and perhaps even a river crossing.

Tonight after supper Mr. Vieux enchanted us for hours with family tales. He knew our grandparents, Mr. **Jean-Baptiste-Point DuSable** and Kittihawa (Catherine), our Potawatomi grandmother. The evening brought many sad and sweet memories.

Bonner Springs, Kansas, May 12

We are at the end of our first day on the road. Yesterday we brought our whole wagon train up by boat from Independence to the Kansas River. We arrived here after an easy afternoon.

People and Terms to Know

Potawatomi—Native American people of the Algonquian language group. In the 1600s, they lived in what is now Wisconsin. They expanded into what is now Michigan, Indiana, and Illinois. In the early 1800s they were forced to sell their land to the U.S. Most moved to a reservation in southern Kansas.

Jean-Baptiste-Point DuSable—(c. 1750–1818) fur trader from Haiti whose trading post on Lake Michigan later became the city of Chicago. He moved to St. Charles, Missouri, around 1800.

Vermilion River, Kansas, May 20

We have reached Mr. Vieux's land, which includes a good <u>ford</u> across the Vermilion River. We will camp here an extra day.

Little Blue River, June 1

This morning at sunrise we saw a huge cloud of dust off to the east. The dust turned out to be a large column of U.S. soldiers and their wagons. They were headed for Fort Kearney. Our men made good wages fixing wheels and wagons. Adela and I did brisk business with the officers' wives.

Near New Fort Kearney, on the Platte River, Nebraska, June 15

We are camped near the place where the trail from Iowa meets our trail from Independence. There a steady stream of wagons poured in from both trails. I never saw such dust, heard such noise, or felt such heat in all my life.

The <u>emigrants</u> look thin, sun-baked, and desperate. Most of them travel on foot. By this time

---

People and Terms to Know

ford—shallow place where it is easy to cross a river or stream. Louis Vieux built a bridge across his ford, charged $1 per crossing, and collected up to $300 a day.

emigrants—people who leave a country to live in another. (Immigrants are people who come into a country.)

they have been on the road for weeks. On good days, they move 15 miles.

Wagons are starting to break apart. Iron stoves were dumped many miles back. People are ready to trade fancy horses and furniture for our good, strong mules. They are buying our oxen at three times Independence prices.

Wagons are starting to break apart. Iron stoves were dumped many miles back.

We trade some of the horses to the Indians, though in truth they have very little left to trade. Last year disease swept through their villages, killing many thousands of them. Poor bands from different tribes now follow the wagon trains, begging for food.

At the Fork of the Platte River, June 27

Today a trapper brought us terrible news from the Oregon Territory. The Cayuse Indians attacked a mission station on the Columbia River. The missionary, **Marcus Whitman**, and his wife are dead. This news has created much alarm all along the trail.

People and Terms to Know

Marcus Whitman—(1802–1847) American missionary and Oregon pioneer. He and his wife were killed in late November 1847.

Across from Chimney Rock, July 4

All around us, noisy celebrations arise from the camps. Anti-Indian feeling has been growing since the news of the Whitman massacre. So we are staying on the north side of the river and standing full guard. A party of **Mormons** has camped nearby. Between the hymns and the fireworks, we'll get very little sleep tonight!

Warm Springs, near Scott's Bluff, Nebraska, July 6

We are setting up a trading post here for several days. I should note that all of our black cloth is gone. People here say a tenth of the emigrants die along the trail.

July 7

This morning I was thinking about business when I heard a voice calling, "Catherine! Catherine!" It was our old trapper friend, **Henri Chatillon**. He is as gallant as ever, though still in deep sorrow over the death of his wife. Their children remain with their mother's tribe. He visits their village whenever he can.

People and Terms to Know

Mormons—members of the Church of Jesus Christ of Latter-day Saints; they founded Salt Lake City in 1847.

Henri Chatillon—French hunter, trapper, and guide who came from the St. Louis area. Francis Parkman wrote about him in his book *The Oregon Trail*.

From Henri we have learned more disturbing news. In tribes from here to Oregon, they talk of attacking the wagon trains. In spite of this, we have decided to go forward. Henri will travel with us.

Fort Laramie, Wyoming, July 15

Everything is in a complete uproar here, and rumors of all kinds are flying. Justin wants to continue west, to learn as much as we can, because our business depends on the Indian trade.

Today he tried to make Adela and me go back home with our baggage and profits. We had a long discussion about it, and we were finally able to change his mind. We agreed that the baggage slows us down, so we decided to leave it in the keeping of traders we trust. Now we will be able to travel much faster.

South Pass, Wyoming, July 30

Today we crossed through the mountains. A group of fur trappers entered our camp this morning in great excitement. They claimed that gold has been discovered in California, and people are striking it rich overnight. This is the wildest rumor we have heard so far!

Soda Springs, Idaho, August 5

Since we left the South Pass, the gold fever has spread. We can see the results from where we are camped, at a high point overlooking the trail. Below us flows a stream of tattered wagons, half-starved cattle, and exhausted people. Then, suddenly, most of the human stream moves to the southwest, in the direction of California. Another stream, much smaller now, continues west to Oregon.

As for us, we are heading home. Justin will probably come back next year, with a much bigger supply train. Henri will command higher prices than ever for his services as a guide. Business prospects look good.

QUESTIONS TO CONSIDER

1. What are some reasons why so many people were traveling on the Oregon Trail?

2. What different groups of people traveled on the Oregon Trail?

3. What kinds of goods and services did travelers on the Oregon Trail need?

4. What events changed life along the Oregon Trail in the summer of 1848?

5. How did the Oregon Trail affect the lives of Indians and fur trappers?

Catherine Haun, traveling west with her husband in 1849, recounts a stop along the Oregon Trail:

It was the fourth of July when we reached the beautiful Laramie River. Its sparkling, pure waters were full of myriads of fish that could be caught with scarcely an effort. It was necessary to build barges to cross the river and during the enforced delay our animals rested and we had one of our periodical "house cleanings." This general systematic re-adjustment always freshened up our wagon train very much, for after a few weeks of travel things got mixed up and untidy and often wagons had to be abandoned if too worn for repairs, and generally one or more animals had died or been stolen.

The California Gold Rush

BY MARY KATHLEEN FLYNN

October 1851

Rich Bar, California

Dear Mother,

You will be happy to hear that Jack and I have arrived safely at our new home. The town, which is really just a mining settlement, is called Rich Bar. It's on the Feather River, and the countryside here is really quite pretty. The California oaks look a little like apple trees in **New England**! Of course the **Sierra Nevada** mountains here are much, much bigger than the hills we have in Massachusetts.

> **People and Terms to Know**
>
> **New England**—section of the northeastern United States that includes the states of Maine, New Hampshire, Vermont, Massachusetts, Connecticut, and Rhode Island.
>
> **Sierra Nevada**—mountain range in California where gold was first discovered in the state.

A woman brings lunch to a team of miners who are using a long tom, a
device in which gravel was washed to separate out gold.

I know you were very sad to see us go west, and I was sad to leave Father and you too. You say Jack and I have gotten **"gold fever,"** and maybe we have. Certainly, Jack has talked of nothing but California for the past three years. Since 1848, when gold was discovered here in the foothills of the Sierra Nevada, Jack has known that he wanted to be part of the **California gold rush**.

We are very tired from our trip. I walked the last five miles! The hill leading into Rich Bar is very steep, and I decided to walk rather than to trust riding on my mule. I know Jack and I will sleep well tonight! I'll write more soon.

From your loving but far-away daughter,
Lilly

Dear Mother,

Jack and I have been in Rich Bar for a week now, and it is a very interesting life we have here. We are living in the Empire Hotel while we wait for our

---

People and Terms to Know

gold fever—desire to get rich quickly from a discovery of gold. The "sickness" spread all over the world like wildfire.

California gold rush—name given to the movement of tens of thousands of people who rushed to the state from all over the world in hopes of making a fortune by finding gold.

own log home to be built. The hotel is the only two-story building in town. It is very fancy—maybe too fancy for plain New Englanders like Jack and me. Just about everything in the hotel is red! But, as fancy as the hotel looks, it is still rough. There is straw on the floor, and the roof isn't a real roof. It's made of canvas!

The hotel is the only two-story building in town.

The bedrooms are all on the second floor. On the first floor is a bar and also a store. Jack and I try to avoid the bar because the men spend most of their time gambling on cards. In a way, everybody here is gambling every day on finding gold.

I do like to spend time in the store downstairs. Everything from ham and oysters to leather and flannel shirts is sold there. The people who come into the shop are fascinating. Almost all of them are men, but they come from all over the world. I've seen people from Mexico, Chile, Spain, and China—and from all parts of the United States.

Life is very exciting here in California, but I do feel homesick. Maybe California will just be an adventure for Jack and me, and maybe we'll make our real home back east after all.

Until then, I remain your loving daughter,
Lilly

Miners build a "corduroy road" out of timbers to cross the Rocky Mountains.

D ear Mother,

Another week has gone by, and the excitement has started to wear off. I feel lonely much of the time—especially since Jack is away from me so much. He is getting more and more frantic to find gold.

Jack has formed a company with five or six other men from New England, and every day they work different spots trying to sift gold from the dirt and rocks. It is back-breaking labor. Every night, Jack comes back to the Empire Hotel tired and dirty and mostly empty-handed. One hole they were working on caved in, and another had to be abandoned because it was flooded.

In the evening, Jack has started to join the men at the bar, though he promises me that he doesn't gamble. Last night, I pointed out to him that he gambles every day at the gold mines. We had our first real fight, and I cried myself to sleep.

I think I would feel less lonely if there were more women here. But until I make a friend, at least I have you, dear Mother, to write to!

I am your loving daughter,
Lilly

Dear Mother,

At last, I have made a friend! She is the wife of a doctor. In fact, her husband, Dr. Clappe, was the first doctor in Rich Bar. There are twenty-nine doctors here now!

Jack told Dr. Clappe he wishes we had come out here a year ago. Indeed, my new friend Mrs. Clappe says that those who worked the mines in the fall of 1850 made their fortunes. Sadly, some of those same lucky souls lost their fortunes at the card tables even faster than they made them!

In fact, at one point, her mule threw her to the ground!

Mrs. Clappe calls herself "**Dame Shirley**." She really is quite elegant, so the name fits her well. She is a bit full of herself, but I find her funny and excellent company.

She told quite a funny story about her journey here from San Francisco. Like Jack and me, she traveled on the back of a mule for much of the trip. In fact, at one point, her mule threw her to the ground!

People and Terms to Know

Dame Shirley—pen name of Louisa Clappe, whose letters to her sister in 1851 and 1852 show what life was like in the California gold mines.

But she just dusted herself off and got back on again. That's the kind of person she is.

Dr. Clappe and Dame Shirley got lost twice on the way here. They spent two nights camped out under the stars with no blankets and no food. She insists they almost got eaten by grizzly bears and bitten by rattlesnakes!

She also said they were lucky they were not attacked by Indians like that French couple who were killed a few months ago. But I think she's being silly. All the Indians I have seen have been peaceful. On the journey to Rich Bar, I saw a group of women carrying baskets and gathering flower seeds, which they mix with acorns and grasshoppers to make bread. They reminded me of the farmers' wives back home at harvest time.

Maybe Dame Shirley stretches the truth a little to make a good story. You know the type of person who can make anything sound exciting. She's a born storyteller. I bet she could make a fortune writing books.

I will write again next week.
Fondly,
Your daughter Lilly

Dear Mother,

As my friend Dame Shirley says, "Gold mining is nature's great **lottery** scheme." I am sorry to report that Jack and I have lost the lottery.

> *I was sound asleep, but I woke up when I heard him crying.*

Last night, Jack came upstairs after spending the evening in the bar. I was sound asleep, but I woke up when I heard him crying. Mother, I had never seen Jack cry before! I asked him what was wrong, and he confessed the truth. What little gold he had found is all gone. He lost everything in a card game!

We spent the whole night talking about it. At first I was very angry and disappointed in him, but by dawn I forgave him. So many men here have fallen sick to the same gold fever—including the two men who found the first gold here at Rich Bar. They are penniless now, like Jack and me.

The good news is that we are coming home! I still have the money Father pressed into my hand

People and Terms to Know

lottery—drawing of lots in which prizes are given to winning numbers or names; also, something decided by chance.

when we left Boston, and that will pay for our journey back east. By the time you get this letter, we will be well on our way!

I remain your faithful, though poorer, daughter,
Lilly

QUESTIONS TO CONSIDER

1. Why did the 1848 discovery of gold in California draw tens of thousands of people to the state?

2. How do you think the gold rush changed towns like Rich Bar?

3. How would you describe "gold fever"?

4. How is searching for gold like gambling?

The California Gold Rush
by R. Conrad Stein

Information and photographs here tell the story of life during the California gold rush.

Hurry Freedom
by Jerry Stanley

Jerry Stanley tells the story of Mifflin Gibbs, a newly freed black slave who marvels at the opportunities before him as he begins to establish a life for himself during the early years of the gold rush. Gibbs is able to start a successful boot and shoe business and, through support of other blacks, lead a movement to obtain equal rights for freed slaves in California.

The Gold Rush
by Bobbie Kalman

Learn about the prospectors' way of life, their tools, and the bustling gold rush towns they lived in. Bobbie Kalman covers one of the most exciting and difficult times in American history in an informative, entertaining book.

The Chisholm Trail

BY BRIAN J. MAHONEY

I don't take kindly to writing, but since I know how and I have a lot of time on my hands, I thought I'd tell the world about my adventures **cowpunching** on the Chisholm Trail.

It all started in a sleepy **saloon** in south Texas. I was playing cards with a gentleman by the name of Diamond Bill Johnson. He was a freed slave, and dressed real flashy—dark suit, silk hat, white tie, and two **six-shooters** to let people know he meant business. (Most cowboys don't wear two guns— they have no need for them. Only gunfighters wear

---

People and Terms to Know

cowpunching—slang for "cowboy work."
saloon—drinking establishment.
six-shooters—handguns that can fire six bullets without reloading.

This trail boss has with him everything he needs for life on a cattle drive.

two guns.) And even though I fought for the South—for TEXAS, I mean—in the Civil War, I never liked slavery much anyway. It just didn't seem right. Most afternoons you could find me and Bill whoopin' it up and taking each other's money.

With a name like Diamond Bill, you wouldn't expect he was a cowboy, but he was. He told me that he got all his gambling money and his fancy clothes by working the Chisholm Trail. After Bill cleaned me out of cash in the early spring of 1871, he gave me a pat on the back and the name of a **cowman** who might hire me for a roundup and drive.

When I rode up, they weren't too glad to see me. Bill had loaned me some gear: a good saddle, **bridle, spurs, chaps**, a pair of blankets, and a Colt .45 six-shooter on my hip. But these were hard-living men who spotted me for a **tenderfoot** right off.

They had already done the spring roundup of the wild longhorn cattle. Now they were **branding** the new calves who were born in the winter and spring. They branded a flying M (an M with little

---

People and Terms to Know

cowman—man who owned land and cattle.

bridle, spurs, chaps—bridles are headgear that help steer the horse; spurs are metal prongs attached to the back of riding boots to urge the horse forward; and chaps are leather leggings worn for riding.

tenderfoot—newcomer to the cowboy life.

branding—burning ownership symbols into an animal's hide.

wings) on its left back leg so a right-handed man could easily see it and rope it. Anyway, they didn't like strangers.

"What do you want, Tenderfoot?" asked the **Trail Boss**. He was not the kind to tip his hat to a lady on the street.

"I'm a friend of Diamond Bill. I'm lookin' for some work drivin' longhorns up to **Abilene**." I said it like I knew what I was saying.

> *"Do you think you can you break a wild horse?"*

After the men laughed a spell, the boss asked, "Do you think you can you break a wild horse?"

"Yep."

"Well, if you can, I'll pay you thirty dollars a month to ride drag. Yer lucky. Longhorns are wilder than most, and I was thinkin' we wouldn't have enough men in the saddle."

I got lucky again when one of the men, a Mexican cowboy called "Loco," took a liking to me. He told me the horse threw the last three men who tried to break him. But, he said, *he* knew how to break him. Well, I broke him—AND nearly broke

---

People and Terms to Know

Trail Boss—boss of a cattle drive.
Abilene—city in Kansas from which cattle were shipped east by train.

---

my back and a few teeth too! Everyone cheered except the Trail Boss—and he didn't like me till I proved myself on the trail.

Anyway, as we started driving the herd north along the trail, Loco (or Carlos, as I called him) told me all I needed to know about being a cowboy. First off, I found out that riding "drag" on the herd is the *worst* place to be and that it was usually saved for the new cowboys in the outfit. Why is it the worst? Drag riders ride behind the herd, and the dust from about 3,000 head of cattle will choke you to *death*. We had to wear bandannas around our faces all the time. We chased the cattle that fell off the herd and pushed the stragglers forward when they lagged behind.

Everybody had a place on our drive up the Chisholm Trail. Mister Trail Boss rode up front because he took care of everything: hiring men and finding the next watering place and camp for the night. He rode first. Then came the cook, who everyone called "Old Lady." He was an old cow-puncher who was like a mother to the men. He cooked up good grub, stitched our britches, and gave us advice—whether we liked it or not! He was like mother, wife, and cowboy rolled into one

▲

Cowboys eat on the range beside their chuck wagon.

because there weren't many women out there. (Why? Most women marry merchants and farmers— not a man who works in a saddle twenty hours a day. Women are too smart for that.)

Anyway, after the Old Lady's grub wagon came the men who ride point (the front of the herd), then the swing riders (out at the "shoulders"), then the flank riders (at the "hips"), and then us dirty drag men holding up the rear.

Well, we moved up the Chisholm Trail at about ten miles a day. It was slow going. You can go faster, but we wanted to give the herd time to graze and fatten up before we got them to the stockyards in Abilene, Kansas. The reason for this drive in the first place is that we have too many head of cattle in Texas. You could only get a few dollars a head if you sold 'em down there. But, in the markets up north, you could get $40 a head! When the railroad was built, they put a stop at Abilene. Some genius figured out that he'd make big money if we drive the cattle north to Abilene and then he ships them to Chicago to meet their Maker.

It was long and boring following a big herd of cattle around.

There's not much to say about life on the trail. It was long and boring following a big herd of cattle around. Sometimes a calf would run off, or we'd cross a river. We'd kill time talking, practicing our trick riding, roping, and the like. But you couldn't ask for a better bunch of men—all of them were tough but good-natured boys. About a third of us were ex-slaves or Mexican, but out there we lived like brothers. I think it's the towns that make people crazy.

The excitement level rose among the boys as we passed through Oklahoma Territory and were moving into Kansas. We didn't have any problems

The Chisholm Trail, 1872

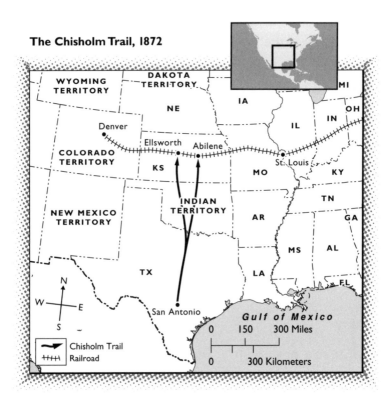

with Indian attacks or cattle rustlers. But one night a storm hit, and when the lightning started, confusion took over. "_Stampede_!!!" someone yelled. Well, I didn't know my hat from a hole in the ground, but I jumped on my horse and rode up front with the rest of the men. It took hours, but

People and Terms to Know

Stampede—group of animals running out of control.

we stopped the cattle at last. The trick in stopping a stampede is to turn the front of the herd around to meet the back of the herd. The cattle start moving in a circle, and the herd soon slows down.

Well, we finally got to the yards in Abilene, and then everything went crazy again. This time it was *us*—wild cowboys loose in a **cow town** with an itch for a good time and lots of pay money to scratch it! And that's how I came to write these words—I had such a good time that I won't be getting out of Abilene jail for a spell. But you can bet your boots you'll find me on the Chisholm Trail again next year!

QUESTIONS TO CONSIDER

1. How would you define the terms *cowman* and *tenderfoot?*
2. What is branding, and why was it done?
3. Who was the Trail Boss, and what did he do?
4. Why did the Chisholm Trail and other cattle-driving trails develop?
5. What do you think attracted men to becoming cowboys on the Chisholm Trail?

People and Terms to Know

cow town—town at the end of a cattle trail. This kind of town normally had wild cowboys and lots of ways for them to spend their money.

Farming on the Great Plains

BY DIANE WILDE

$\mathbf{M}$ary knew that life as a farmer's wife in the new territories would be difficult. But nothing she had experienced growing up in Philadelphia could have prepared her for the harsh reality of this land. The sun seemed to beat down much hotter here on the **prairie** than it had in Pennsylvania. They had traveled for four days without seeing a tree before they finally found the slow, narrow creek where they staked their **claim**. Near the stream, a few oak trees struggled to survive in the hot prairie winds.

Mary and Frank had been married for one year when Frank decided he wanted to farm his own

---

People and Terms to Know

prairie—wide, flat, largely treeless grasslands, such as the Great Plains of central North America.

claim—piece of land a homesteader takes ownership of; the area of the land is defined by stakes, or pegs, driven into the ground.

A family stands beside their wagon on the way to a farmstead on the land. They had been living with Frank's uncle on his farm in western Pennsylvania. Little available farm land remained east of the Mississippi— certainly none that Frank could afford. So the couple had decided to go west, where plenty of land could be had.

As they traveled westward, both Frank and Mary began to become aware of the challenges they faced. A few days after they stopped and made camp, Mary wrote to her family to let them know that she and Frank had arrived safely.

June 23, 1884

Dear Mother and Father,

Frank and I have finally found our piece of land. We are in **Nebraska** just south of the **Platte River**. Seward is the nearest town. The journey was long and difficult, and I am happy to stop traveling at last. You can't even imagine what the country is like here! It is so different from what I am used to back home. The land stretches out forever in all directions with

---

People and Terms to Know

Nebraska—state in the central United States, in the Great Plains.
Platte River—river in southern Nebraska.

nothing but prairie grasses waving in the wind, and the wind never stops blowing. The earth is almost flat, with only low rolling hills. For me, the worst thing is the lack of trees. We often traveled for days without seeing even one tree. A person can find almost no shade out here, and it is getting hotter every day.

Out here, people make their houses out of the hard, root-matted prairie soil.

We were extremely lucky to find a spot by a little creek with a few small oak trees along the banks. We are camping by the creek in our wagon now while we build a little **sod house**. Out here, people make their houses out of the hard, root-matted prairie soil. We cut the sod into squares and stack them like bricks. The lack of trees means lumber is scarce and has to be shipped in from far away. A wood frame house is so expensive it is out of the question for us right now. Most of the settlers here live in these rather dull little sod houses. I dream that we can build a nicer house once our farm is going strong.

We have very little water, and fuel for fires is hard to come by. To build our campfire at night, we

---

People and Terms to Know

sod house—house made from chunks of earth and straw.

A Great Plains farm family of the 1880s stands in front of their sod house.

collect grasses and dried buffalo dung, called *chips*, from the nearby prairie. We have to be very careful with fire, because the wind can easily blow a spark into the dry grass and set it aflame. We saw several large fires burning for miles on the prairie during our journey.

Settlers who have been here a few years are filling my ears with tales of the hardships of living out here. Two years ago, huge clouds of grasshoppers came out of the sky and began to eat the grain and almost everything else in their path. I'm beginning to wonder if we will make a go of it here.

I miss you all very much and hope everyone is well. I will write again soon.

Love, Mary

August 15, 1884

Dear Folks,

Our little house is finished now, but it is certainly not much to look at. The back of the house is dug into a low hill and the rest, made from pieces of sod, pokes out in the front. It has only one window, so it seems quite dark inside, and it is impossible to keep it clean. The wind blows little bits of dirt from the cracks between the sod chunks, and dust gets on everything. Not that we have much in the way of furniture—just a table, two wobbly chairs, and our bed. Our crude wooden bed sits right on the dirt floor. The one big advantage of the house is that it stays fairly cool inside. That is a great comfort because the days are hotter than ever lately.

The good news is that I am expecting our first child. I am very happy, but I have seen how difficult it is here for women with children. There aren't very many women out here, and it has been hard for me to find friends to talk with. Last week I walked almost three miles to the nearest neighbor's place to introduce myself. The poor woman there has four children, all under the age of seven. She is alone with them most of the time because her husband is working their farm. The children are restless and fussy because there isn't much for them to do. Besides, it is too hot for them to play outside for very long.

Last week I walked almost three miles to the nearest neighbor's place to introduce myself.

I hope you are well, and I'll write again soon.
Your loving daughter, Mary

October 12, 1884

My dear friend Emily,

I miss you so much. You can't imagine what my life is like here. I so desperately need to talk honestly with someone I can trust. I have no close friends here, and I don't want my folks to know how really miserable I am. That will just make them worry more than they already do, so please don't pass on any of what I am about to tell you.

I am so terribly lonely here by myself. Frank is away working the farm from sunrise to sunset. The houses are spread so far apart that I sometimes go days without seeing another person except Frank. When he gets home, he hardly has a word to say, he is so tired.

My mother may have told you that I am expecting a baby in early spring. The sickness of the first few months has let up. But I am still very tired and I have to work all day long to get the chores done. I had to tend our vegetable garden all summer. Lately, I've been saving some of the harvest. I also feed the chickens, collect eggs, milk the cow, and carry water from the creek. It started to run dry at the end of August, but fortunately we got some much needed rain in early September.

I'm worried that we won't have enough wood to burn to get through the winter.

Most frustrating of all is the constant battle with dirt and dust. We battled the dust here all summer. Now the nights are getting cold, and I'm worried that we won't have enough wood to burn to get through the winter. I miss the comforts of Philadelphia so horribly. If I didn't love Frank so much, I would return east as soon as possible. Please write and tell me how you are and what is happening in the lovely city of Philadelphia these days.

Your loving friend, Mary

*   *   *

Mary and Frank barely made it through the bitter winter cold and the terrible storms. The blizzards swept across the plains like nothing they had ever seen before. But at last, spring came, and with it came their new baby girl. Spring also brought new neighbors. Two more farms sprang up nearby, and the couple found friends among their neighbors. Then Mary's younger brother James decided to come for the summer to help Frank with the farming. With the extra help and the new friends, the coming year promised to be better than last year. Mary and Frank decided to stick it out for another year.

QUESTIONS TO CONSIDER

1. Why did people such as Mary and Frank go west?

2. Why did they need to be so careful with fire?

3. What caused Mary to be unhappy? How do you think you would feel in her situation?

4. How was Mary's life on the prairie different from her life in Philadelphia?

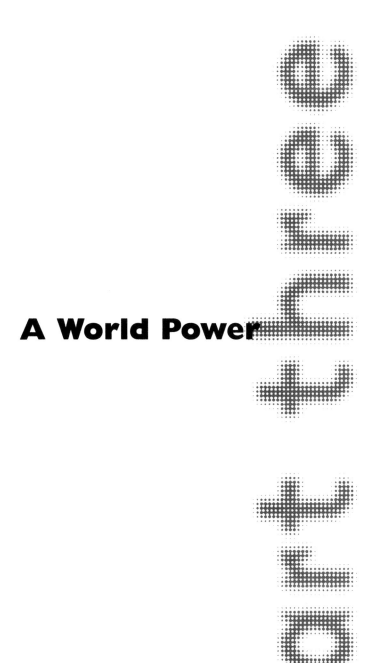

A World Power

The Opening of Japan

BY BARBARA LITTMAN

Dateline: March 31, 1854
Kanagawa, Japan. On March 31, **Commodore Matthew Perry** signed a Treaty of Friendship with Japan in the coastal town of **Kanagawa**. Perry's success came almost nine months after his mission in July of last year. At that time, he delivered a letter from **President Fillmore** asking the Japanese government to allow trade. He also wanted a place in the Pacific Ocean where ships could be refueled.

People and Terms to Know

Commodore Matthew Perry—(1794–1858) commander of the U.S. fleet that opened Japan to trade with the United States in 1854. He was the son of a distinguished sea captain and brother of Oliver Hazard Perry, naval officer in the War of 1812.

Kanagawa—Japanese city where the first treaty between Japan and the United States was signed.

President Fillmore—(1800–1874) Millard Fillmore, U.S. president from 1850 to 1853. He sent Commodore Perry to open trade relations with Japan.

立浪や玉をちらして
笘が山 船の車の
くるくるりくるり辻

花 陰
(印)

(印)

In this Japanese print, a father and son look at one of the ships of the American fleet.

The treaty falls far short of the trade agreement the U.S. wanted. However, it represents an important first step with Japan. This island has closed itself off from the outside world for more than two hundred years.

Japan has agreed to rescue shipwrecked American sailors and treat them well.

The treaty says that American whaling and trading ships can stop in Japan to refuel and buy supplies. The agreement came after Perry's threat of attack and weeks of talks between Perry, his aides, and Japanese officials. In addition to the refueling **provision**, three other important agreements were won by the Americans. Japan has agreed to rescue shipwrecked American sailors and treat them well. Japan agreed to open the ports of **Shimoda and Hakodate** to American ships, and it agreed to allow an American **consul** to live in Shimoda at either country's request. More promising for a possible trade agreement between the two

People and Terms to Know

provision—clause or passage in a document or agreement.

Shimoda and Hakodate—two of the first Japanese port towns to be opened to American ships that needed supplies and fuel.

consul—official appointed by a government to live in a foreign city and represent his or her government's interests there.

countries is that Japan named the United States as a **most favored nation**.

*　　*　　*

"Well, that might be the news," thought Charles Malotte as he dipped his pen in the ink one last time, "but it's sure not the story."

He couldn't spend any more time on his news story. Just the bare facts would have to do. The ship that was going to take the story back to the United States, and to his editor in San Francisco, was leaving soon. Quickly, Charles scribbled a note letting his editor know more would be coming. Shoving the papers in an envelope, he dashed up to the deck and handed the package to the messenger who was waiting for it.

"What a day," Charles muttered as he leaned against the ship's railing, staring out at the broad-sailed Japanese fishing boats bobbing in the bay. Then he laughed. "Really, I should say what a month. I've seen things I never thought I would see in my lifetime."

People and Terms to Know

most favored nation—country with the best trading terms the importing nation gives. Imports from countries named "most favored nation" are taxed less heavily than goods from other countries.

It was a stroke of luck that Charles Malotte was even standing on deck, gazing out at this mysterious island country. How his editor had arranged this assignment was something Charles would never know. Somehow, his editor had convinced Commodore Perry he needed a journalist on board to report on the success he would achieve.

"Well," thought Charles, "maybe it was all done through flattery, but the Commodore has certainly kept his end of the bargain. He's given me several long interviews and allowed me to observe all the talks and the final treaty signing. Perry has had a remarkable success. Other countries have failed to make a treaty with Japan. Commodore Perry is the only one who succeeded, and he did it peacefully too."

Charles had come to respect Perry during their weeks together aboard the _Powhatan_. Commodore Perry looked tall and stern, but he was a fair man. He had great intelligence and an even greater sense of curiosity. As far as Charles was concerned, these

---

People and Terms to Know

Powhatan—sailing vessel in Perry's squadron that was used as the meeting and banquet area during Perry's trip to Japan.

traits made him the perfect interview candidate. Even in short interviews with Perry, Charles ended up with more information than he often got in hours of conversation with other people.

Charles would never forget his first conversation with the Commodore. They had been standing on deck. Whales and porpoises swam around the

The Japanese had taken it as a sure sign that they were being invaded by barbarians.

bow of the ship. Charles knew the Commodore had delivered a letter from President Fillmore the previous July to representatives of the Emperor. What he hadn't known about was the greeting Perry had received.

Perry had laughed when he described the meteor that had streaked through the sky the night they arrived. The Japanese had taken it as a sure sign that they were being invaded by **barbarians**. That night, the temples were filled with people praying that Japan would be spared.

People and Terms to Know

barbarians—people considered by another group to be primitive and without culture.

北里墨利加合衆国
洪和政治洲
上官真像之写

釜左全権国王侯筆
海軍水師提督某々々

壬城火都府
筆墨頼通
四千五百里
海七十八日之
日本之渡来

嘉富神奈

武州本牧撞資
上陸應對之図写

Several days later, Perry and his crew were amazed to see their ships surrounded by small Japanese boats. Perry smiled when he described the scene. The boats weren't filled with soldiers bearing arms, but rather with artists bearing brushes. Later, he and his men learned that the pictures the artists created were being copied and sold with the caption "Hairy Barbarians."

Yet, the first meeting had been civil. The Commodore delivered the president's letter, stored safely in a beautiful rosewood box with gold hinges. In response, the Japanese gave Perry a document saying the letter would be delivered to the

Emperor. Of course, no one knew then that it would really be delivered to the **Shogun**. Then the Japanese asked Perry to leave. Only nine days after his arrival, Commodore Perry turned his fleet around, telling the Japanese he would return in the spring to receive the Emperor's response.

"And that's why there was a second voyage and I ended up getting to see sights most Americans can only dream of," Charles thought.

First, just the sight of snowcapped Mt. Fuji as they pulled into Tokyo Bay was like nothing Perry had ever seen. And the sight of the Japanese filling their sleeves with leftover food after the first banquet still made him smile. Of course, the Americans had to do the same when the Japanese invited them to a banquet several days later. It would have been impolite not to do so.

Certainly the days had been filled with boredom during the many weeks of waiting for the Japanese response, but they brought adventures, too. Every day, small American boats went out

People and Terms to Know

Shogun—true ruler of Japan at the time of Perry's missions. The Emperor was only a ceremonial figure. The word *Shogun* means "barbarian-expelling general" in Japanese.

charting the waters off Japan, and Charles tried to join them whenever he could. Commodore Perry also arranged to show American technology to the Japanese. What an amusing sight it was to see a **samurai** warrior riding the small-scale train along its 350-foot track. Japanese runners also raced against a Morse code telegraph to try to beat the telegraph at getting messages from one place to another.

After all the waiting, even Commodore Perry became restless.

After all the waiting, even Commodore Perry became restless. He commanded his ships to sail for the capital, **Edo**. The Japanese had just sent **Kayama** to meet with Perry. Commodore Perry and Kayama knew each other from Perry's previous trip. Kayama convinced the Commodore that sailing to Edo would be a national disgrace for the Japanese. If they were disgraced, there would be no treaty.

People and Terms to Know

samurai—belonging to the military class of Japan. Japanese warriors were expected to be scholars as well as soldiers. They organized the work of the farming, artisan, and merchant classes in Japan.

Edo—now Tokyo, Japan's capital.

Kayama—Kayama Yezaiman, Japanese official chosen by the Shogun to negotiate relations between Japan and Perry on both of Perry's visits.

Perry agreed to a meeting in the small coastal town of Kanagawa. The Japanese hurriedly constructed a special treaty house where the signing would take place.

"Now that was a sight I'll never forget," Charles continued his train of thought.

The treaty house itself looked like a coal shed. It was decorated, though, with colorful streamers and tassels. A group of samurai soldiers dressed in their colorful clothing stood guard at the entrance. Not to be outdone, Perry arrived with 500 of his men and three marching bands. As he was escorted into the treaty house, he had his men perform a 21-gun salute to honor the Emperor and a 17-gun salute to honor the advisers who represented him.

The rest of the meeting was boring. Translators had to be used. At one point, Perry had to speak English to his interpreter, who then spoke Dutch to the Emperor's representative, who then translated that into Japanese. Finally, Commodore Perry received a long scroll in reply to President Fillmore's letter.

"It's hard to believe I witnessed this," thought Charles. "Building relations with Japan has to be one of the most historic events of the century, and I saw it all."

Completely lost in thought, Charles hadn't heard **George Preble** approach. "Charles," he said, "they're arriving now. The Commodore wants us to outdo ourselves. This will be the banquet to end all banquets. The Japanese must remember us for our hospitality."

Hurrying after him, Charles could only think about how glad he was they were hosting the banquet. He wouldn't go so far as to say he hated raw fish and saki, but he certainly preferred the dishes he knew the Commodore's French chef prepared.

QUESTIONS TO CONSIDER

1. What benefits did the United States receive from Japan when the Treaty of Friendship was signed?

2. What is your opinion of the success of Perry's second mission? What additional benefits had he hoped to negotiate with Japan?

3. How did the Japanese view the arrival of Perry and his ships?

4. Why was the signing of the Treaty of Friendship an important historical event?

People and Terms to Know

George Preble—George Henry Preble (1816–1885), was a lieutenant on Perry's expedition to Japan. His letters to his wife provide an excellent record of the mission.

Some of the American Presents for the Japanese

For the Emperor:

- Miniature steam engine, 1/4 size, with track, tender, and car.

- 2 telegraph sets, with batteries, three miles of wire, gutta percha [rubber-like substance] wire, and insulators.

- 1 Francis's copper lifeboat.

- 1 surfboat of copper.

- Collection of agricultural implements.

- *Audubon's Birds*, in nine volumes.

- *Natural History of the State of New York*, 16 volumes.

- *Annals of Congress*, 4 volumes.

- *Laws and Documents of the State of New York*.

- *Journal of the Senate and Assembly of New York*.

- *Lighthouse Reports*, 2 volumes.

- *Bancroft's History of the United States*, 4 volumes.

- Morris, *Engineering*.

- *Farmers' Guide*, 2 volumes.

- 1 series of United States Coast Survey Charts.

- Silver-topped dressing case.

- 8 yards of scarlet broadcloth, and scarlet velvet.

- Series of United States standard yard, gallon, bushel, balances and weights.

- Quarter cask of Madeira [wine].

- Barrel of whiskey.

- Box of champagne and cherry cordial and maraschino.
- 3 boxes of fine tea.
- Maps of several states and four large lithographs.
- Telescope and stand, in box.
- Sheet-iron stove.
- An assortment of fine perfume.
- 5 Hall rifles.
- 3 Maynard muskets.
- 12 cavalry swords.
- 6 artillery swords.
- 1 carbine.
- 20 Army pistols in a box.
- *Catalogue of New York State Library and of Post Offices.*

For the Empress:
- Flowered silk embroidered dress.
- Toilet dressing-box gilded.
- 6 dozen assorted perfumes.

Some of the Japanese Presents for the Americans

1st. For the Government of the United States of America, from the Emperor:

- 1 gold lacquered pen.
- 1 gold lacquered paper box.
- 1 gold lacquered book case.
- 1 lacquered writing table.
- 1 censer [incense-burner] of bronze (cow-shape), supporting silver flower and stand.
- 1 flower holder and stand.
- 2 braziers [charcoal-burners].
- 10 pieces fine red silk.
- 10 pieces white silk.
- 5 pieces flowered silk.

2nd. From Hayashi, 1st commisioner:

- 1 lacquered pen.
- 1 lacquered paper box.
- 1 box of paper.
- 1 box flowered note paper.
- 5 boxes stamped note and letter paper.
- 4 boxes assorted sea shells, 100 in each.
- 1 box of branch coral and feather in silver.
- 1 lacquered chow-chow [preserved fruit] box.
- 1 box, set of three, lacquered goblets.
- 7 boxes cups and spoons and goblet cut from conch shells.

A Hawaiian Speaks of His Last Queen

BY DEE MASTERS

Where the palm trees sway and near the clear waters of Waimea Bay lie the white beaches of Hawaii. The beautiful 'ahihi flower in the forest is woven by the winds into your **lei**. Its sweet aroma comes to us today, Queen **Liliuokalani**, last queen of Hawaii. You steered our little canoe most skillfully, though you were troubled by the many small birds that tried to cause us pain. In the end, the waves were too great for our little canoe. We cannot always come through. I will always remember you, Queen of your people's hearts, singer of songs. You

---

People and Terms to Know

lei—necklace, usually made of flowers.
Liliuokalani—(1838–1917) last queen of Hawaii; she ruled from 1891 to 1893.

Photograph of former Hawaiian queen Liliuokalani taken in 1916.

and your people of yesterday and today are strung together, like an unfading garland of love.

The rich men, sons of **missionaries**, took our ways from us. They said that our dance, the hula, was wrong. They tried to make us ashamed of what we wore, of our stories and our songs. They said our gods were no more.

Only those who were rich and owned land had a say.

In 1887, King **Kalakaua** was forced to sign a new constitution for our islands. The Hawaiian League, which made him sign, had 405 members, but not one of those members had a name like mine, for none was Hawaiian. They were sons of missionaries, businessmen, and planters of sugarcane. They organized rifle companies while King Kalakaua composed songs. We called the new constitution the "Bayonet Constitution." It took away the voting rights of most Hawaiians. Only those who were rich and owned land had a say.

In our hurt and anger we rose up against these men. One hundred fifty Hawaiian men took over

---

People and Terms to Know

missionaries—people who come into a country to do religious or charity work.
Kalakaua—David Kalakaua (1836–1891), ruler of Hawaii from 1874 to 1891, older brother of Liliuokalani.

Iolani Palace and all the government buildings. We were fired upon, but we held our positions. We were brave, but only a fool builds a sand wall to stop the sea. The League called on U. S. Marines from an American warship. American soldiers responded, killing seven Hawaiians and wounding twelve more. The "Bayonet Constitution" stood. King Kalakaua's power fell.

In 1891, King Kalakaua died, and his sister Liliuokalani became queen. This time was like a storm at sea. Many dangerous currents lay hidden beneath a wild surface. From Molokai, from Kohala, from every district, **petitions** came to the queen calling for a new constitution.

Rumors flew like seabirds frightened by the storm. Some said that white men who were not married to Hawaiians would not be allowed to vote. Others said that our new queen would give the islands to the British rather than let Americans continue to tell her what to do. On January 14, 1893, the queen announced that she would issue a

---

People and Terms to Know

Iolani Palace—royal residence of Hawaii.
petitions—formal letters of request signed by many people.

new constitution. In it, she would return rights to her people.

Alas, that afternoon the leaders of the **missionary party** drew up their plans to overthrow the queen. They called her a traitor for making a new constitution. So, then, what did *they* do? They made a new constitution. Who was the traitor, I ask you? Her constitution was wrong, they said. Their constitution was right, they said. The issue may not have been right or wrong but that they were white and she was brown. In the revolutionary committee, there were five born Americans, four Hawaiian-born sons of American missionaries, one **Tasmanian**, one Scotsman, one German, and no Hawaiians.

On January 15, the revolutionary committee met with the American minister to Hawaii, **John L. Stevens**. He offered to send troops from the

People and Terms to Know

missionary party—political leaders of the settlers in Hawaii. These were mostly Americans whose parents had been missionaries.

Tasmanian—native of Tasmania, island state of southeast Australia.

John L. Stevens—(1820–1895) U.S. minister to Hawaii who helped overthrow Queen Liliuokalani by recognizing the revolutionary government and requesting U.S. troops to protect U.S. citizens and property.

U. S. S. *Boston* against the queen. Justice **Sanford Dole** of the Hawaii Supreme Court was to be the head of their new government. At first, Justice Dole refused, but Stevens, the American minister, persuaded him that the U. S. would make Hawaii a state right away.

On January 16, Minister Stevens ordered American sailors and marines ashore. They camped near the palace.

On January 17, a group of Hawaiian policemen tried to stop a wagon loaded with ammunition for the revolutionaries. One of the revolutionaries shot a policeman in the shoulder. At three o'clock, while people gathered to see what had happened, the revolutionaries took over the government building. At the police station, the police chief refused to give up the building without orders from the queen.

At five o'clock, U. S. Minister Stevens sent a letter to Judge Dole saying that the U. S. recognized the new government as the real government of Hawaii. Stevens had the Hawaiian flag taken down. The American flag was raised over the post office.

People and Terms to Know

Sanford Dole—(1844–1926) American lawyer and political leader in Hawaii. He was born in Honolulu and educated in the U.S. Head of the revolutionary government and president of the Republic of Hawaii, he became the first governor of Hawaii.

At six o'clock, the queen was placed under arrest in her bedroom in the palace. She surrendered—not, she said, to the revolutionaries but to the "superior force of the United States of America." At that moment she believed that when the American president and people learned the facts, she would be restored to power.

In fact, later in the year (1893), President Cleveland removed Minister Stevens and had the American flag taken down. United States Secretary of State Gresham said that the affair reflected badly on the U. S. Liliuokalani begged her people to act peacefully.

But our queen had enemies. The liars said that she wasn't Hawaiian. They said her father had really been a black man, that she worshipped the old gods, that she would behead those who had gone against her. Queen Liliuokalani wrote in one of her songs:

> "Be quiet, you birds who talk about me.
> You are nothing, in my opinion, Yes, indeed.
> You talk of the faults of others, yet there is an
>   evil goddess
> in your chest that you feed with human
>   sacrifices."

▲

On August 12, 1898, the American flag was flown over Iolani Palace, the former royal residence of Queen Liliuokalani, to mark the transfer of Hawaii to the United States.

Our queen never stopped trying to defend her people. She went to Washington. She wrote and spoke for our interests. She offered her own life in defense of those who stood by her. Two years later she was arrested for plotting to overthrow the government that had overthrown her. She was imprisoned for eight months. In prison she continued to write beautiful poems about our land.

She offered her own life in defense of those who stood by her.

In the end, our Queen Liliuokalani was forced to sign a paper saying she was no longer the queen. She was told that if she did not sign, 200 men who had supported her would be killed. She signed.

Our queen was finally released. She was honored by her people and was asked to attend Hawaiian official events until her death at age 79 in 1917. But Hawaii had lost its independence. Queen Liliuokalani did not attend the ceremony when the Hawaiian flag was lowered for the last time and the American flag was officially raised.

QUESTIONS TO CONSIDER

1. According to the narrator, who opposed Queen Liliuokalani and why?

2. What was wrong with the "Bayonet Constitution"?

3. Where did the revolutionaries get their real power?

4. Why did U.S. Secretary of State Gresham have the American flag taken down?

African-American Troops in Cuba

BY JUDITH CONAWAY

Sam was hotter than he'd ever been in his whole life. Even up here on deck, there was no breeze. Sweat poured down his body. His wool uniform itched like crazy. Still, Sam stood at attention. He was proud to be in the U. S. Army and prouder still to be a "**buffalo soldier**."

Sam belonged to Troop D of the **Tenth United States Cavalry**. The Tenth had fought the Apaches

---

People and Terms to Know

buffalo soldier—name given by the Plains Indians to African Americans who served in the U.S. Army.

Tenth United States Cavalry—one of four regiments of African American soldiers in the U.S. Army. All four regiments of "buffalo soldiers" fought at Santiago, Cuba, during the Spanish-American War.

The African-American troops of the U.S. 10th Cavalry Regiment charge at the Battle of San Juan Hill, July 1, 1898.

in the West. Sam had served under Lieutenant **J.J. Pershing**—"Black Jack" himself. Now he and Black Jack had come to Cuba on the very same ship! Sam stood even taller.

I t was June 22, 1898. For the past week, Sam and his fellow soldiers had been at sea. Their steamboat, the *Leona*, had sailed with 31 other ships from Tampa, Florida, to the east coast of Cuba. The ships were loaded with horses, equipment, and soldiers—American and Cuban, black and white.

Sam had spent most of the journey in the **hold**, along with the other black soldiers. They were not allowed to mix with the white troops up on the deck. Down below there was hardly any air, and the smell from the horses made you gag. Some of the men said it was little better than in slave days and wondered why they were fighting a "white man's war."

But the horrible crossing was behind them now. They had reached Cuba. It was time to land and do the job they'd come to do.

People and Terms to Know

J.J. Pershing—John Joseph Pershing (1860–1948), white U.S. army officer nicknamed "Black Jack" for his pride in his black troops. He served in Cuba and the Philippines, and later, in World War I, he commanded American forces in Europe.

hold—below-deck storage area of a ship.

The mission of this **Spanish-American War** was to free the people of Cuba from Spain. So far, the mission had not gone well. The army wasn't prepared for war. The troops had been in Tampa for weeks waiting for ships that came late and for supplies that never came at all. (That was why they were wearing wool uniforms in this blazing heat.)

So far, the mission had not gone well.

During Sam's first week in Cuba, things didn't get much better. First of all, they didn't have nearly enough to eat. The men sweated through days that were beastly hot. In a haze of heat, they slowly unloaded the troop ships. Everything was in confusion.

At last the soldiers began to move inland. By June 30, the Tenth Cavalry had set up camp on a hill near an old plantation. Just half a mile away, they could see the long ridge that guarded the city of Santiago. The ridge had two peaks, San Juan Hill and Kettle Hill. The whole ridge was heavily fortified with guns and ammunition. The American

People and Terms to Know

Spanish-American War—(1898) short war between the United States and Spain. The war began over Cuba, but spread to Puerto Rico, Guam, and the Philippines as well. The U.S. acquired all these islands after the war.

troops had no campfires that night so that they would not be seen by the enemy.

The Spanish attack began early the next morning, July 1. Guns from the ridge pounded down on the Americans. The Spanish guns used smokeless powder, so no one could see where they were located. The Americans had old guns that made puffs of smoke as they were fired.

Bad planning by the army put the troops in danger. Black Jack Pershing was ordered to move the Tenth along a road next to the San Juan River. Several other regiments had received the same orders. The narrow road was so crowded that the troops could barely move.

Worst of all, an American observation balloon floated right above the troops, showing the Spaniards exactly where to direct their fire. Officers were riding back and forth, shouting orders, but no one obeyed because there was too much noise to hear them and too much dust to see them. It was terrifying, and Troop D was right in the middle.

Somehow, army discipline took over from the fear and confusion. Buffalo soldiers from the Ninth and Tenth Cavalries were positioned along the San

Juan River, with the **Rough Riders** between them. The all-white Sixth Infantry lay just behind the Ninth Cavalry. Other regiments, including the all-black Twenty-fourth and Twenty-fifth Infantry Regiments, spread out below the ridge.

Troop D moved into the woods, an area covered by high bushes. Their scouts began crawling away from the others and shooting. They were trying to get the enemy to fire at them so that the others could move ahead. **Corporal John Walker** was the most daring scout, but Sam did his share too.

The Americans crept up the lower slopes of the ridge. Spanish bullets whistled around them. In the thick of the fighting, troops from the various regiments got all mixed up. When they couldn't find their own units, men joined the nearest one, black or white.

B y early afternoon, the Americans had filled the woods. From the woods to the top of the ridge lay only tall grass. If they advanced, they would be in

---

People and Terms to Know

Rough Riders—popular nickname of the First Volunteer Cavalry, led by Theodore Roosevelt.

Corporal John Walker—African-American soldier from Troop D, Tenth U.S. Cavalry. He received the Congressional Medal of Honor for his part in this battle.

clear view of the Spanish rifles. They waited for orders from their superior officers.

No orders came. Spanish **snipers** picked off anyone who stood up. It was so hot many men fainted. Sam felt the panic returning. Finally, one officer had had enough.

Spanish snipers picked off anyone who stood up.

Lieutenant Jules Ord, of the Sixth Infantry, leaped out of the woods. He had a rifle in one hand and a pistol in the other. "Follow me!" he yelled. "We can't stay here!" The lieutenant charged to the top of the ridge. Corporal Walker and other men from Troop D were right behind him.

Cheers and battle cries rose from every American throat. The troops surged forward, holding their rifles above their heads and firing up toward the Spanish snipers.

Lieutenant Ord and Corporal Walker were the first to reach the top of San Juan Hill. A sniper killed Lieutenant Ord, but Corporal Walker killed the sniper. More men swarmed forward, to take and try to hold the hill.

People and Terms to Know

snipers—hidden riflemen.

These African-American soldiers were stationed at Camp Wikoff in New Jersey following service in Cuba during the Spanish-American War. Many of the U.S. troops that served in Cuba came down with tropical diseases and stayed at Camp Wikoff until they recovered.

Theodore Roosevelt and his Rough Riders charged up Kettle Hill. Black Jack Pershing charged with them, leading both buffalo soldiers and white troops. The troops captured Kettle Hill. Then they rode to rescue the troops who were barely holding on at San Juan Hill.

People and Terms to Know

Theodore Roosevelt—(1858–1919) writer, cowboy, soldier, and politician, Roosevelt got most of the credit for the victory at San Juan Hill. He served as governor of New York and as vice president under President William McKinley. When McKinley was assassinated in 1901, Roosevelt became president at the age of 42. He served as the 26th U.S. president until 1909.

By 7:30 that evening, on July 1, the entire ridge was in American hands. But the fighting and the misery went on far longer. The men dug trenches and held off Spanish sniper fire. On July 3, they heard the guns of American ships bombarding Spanish ships in Santiago's harbor. Santiago surrendered on July 17, 1898.

By that time, Sam, like many other American soldiers, had fallen sick with **yellow fever**. It had begun to rain, and water filled the trenches and brought out the mos-

Men were too weak from hunger to resist the disease.

quitoes. Men were too weak from hunger to resist the disease. Four times as many men died from yellow fever than were killed in the fighting. Sam was one of the lucky ones.

*   *   *

Almost twenty years later, another war was being fought, this time in Europe. Black Jack Pershing, now a general, recruited African Americans to join the fighting of World War I. Sam was proud to help him by telling about the black heroes of the Battle of Santiago.

People and Terms to Know

yellow fever—highly infectious tropical disease that is spread by mosquito bites.

"Now, I know some of you are saying this is a white man's war," he told his audiences. "But if you say it's a white man's war, then you have to say this is a white man's country. And I'm saying it's not the white man's country. It's everybody's country. And we're going to charge together to victory, black and white, until there is liberty and justice for all."

QUESTIONS TO CONSIDER

1. What were the four regiments of "buffalo soldiers"?
2. How were black soldiers in the U.S. Army treated differently from white soldiers?
3. What was the mission of the American troops in the Spanish-American War?
4. How did bad planning by the army hurt the efforts of its troops in the field?
5. Why did yellow fever kill so many soldiers?

The Debate Over the Philippines

BY JANE LEDER

I never cared very much for stories about war. But that changed in 1895, when Cuban revolutionaries rose up against the Spanish who had ruled their country for hundreds of years. The Cuban story made exciting reading. Every day the newspaper headlines told of the unrest in Cuba.

Spanish, Cuban, and American **diplomats** began meeting to solve their differences. Maybe they would have solved them if the U. S. battleship *Maine* hadn't sailed into the harbor at Havana, Cuba, on February 15, 1898 and exploded. Two hundred and sixty American sailors were killed.

People and Terms to Know

diplomats—government representatives.

The 20th Kansas Volunteers fought at Caloocan in the Philippines on

The headline of the *New York Journal* that day read: "Destruction of the War Ship *Maine* Was the Work of an Enemy." A team of American experts said the *Maine* had hit a **mine** put there by the Spanish. We Americans went wild and demanded war.

President William McKinley wanted no part of another war. He had fought in the **Civil War**, and he knew the horrors of death and injury. But Americans started to call McKinley a coward. He finally gave in, and America declared war on Spain.

The first battle of the war did not take place in Cuba. It took place in the **Philippines**. On the eve of the war, six American ships that were docked in **Hong Kong** left for the Philippines. They destroyed the Spanish fleet at the capital city of Manila without losing one American.

People and Terms to Know

mine—explosive device used to destroy enemy personnel or equipment, often designed to be set off by contact.

President William McKinley—William McKinley (1843–1901), president of the United States from 1896 to 1901. He urged Congress to enter the Spanish-American War and gained the Philippines for the United States as well as control of Cuba.

Civil War—(1861–1865) war in the United States between the North (the Union) and the South (the Confederacy).

Philippines—country in southeast Asia made up of more than 7,000 islands in the South China and Philippine Seas.

Hong Kong—special administrative region of China, formerly a British colony, located in southeast China on the South China Sea.

On a hot July evening in 1898, I sat in my parlor, reading the *New York Journal*. That day, fighting had taken place in Cuba. Luck was on our side. The Spanish fleet had been trapped in **Santiago Bay** by American warships. The Spanish ships sailed right into the guns of the Americans. All of the Spanish ships were sunk, and 1,800 Spaniards died. We lost just one sailor!

Luck was on our side.

Spain was losing the war. On December 10, 1898, Spain and the United States signed the Treaty of Paris. The treaty ended the war between the two countries. Spain recognized Cuba's independence. She "gave" **Guam** and **Puerto Rico** to the United States. The United States then paid Spain $20 million for giving up the Philippines.

Many Americans like myself supported the Treaty of Paris. However, a small group remained very unhappy. They didn't think America should rule other countries, particularly the Philippines.

People and Terms to Know

Santiago Bay—harbor in Santiago, Cuba.

Guam—largest and southernmost island of the Mariana island group in the Pacific Ocean. Guam is approximately 6,000 miles west of San Francisco.

Puerto Rico—islands between the Caribbean Sea and North Atlantic Ocean, east of the Dominican Republic. Puerto Rico is about 1,000 miles southeast of Miami, Florida.

An organization called the **Anti-Imperialist League** was formed. Its members were against the United States forcing its government on the people of the Philippines, or anywhere else.

Anger filled the islands as well. Filipinos did not want to accept being ruled by another country. They wanted to be free to form their own nation.

My friend Susan joined the Anti-Imperialist League. "The people of the Philippines weren't given a choice," she said. "We wanted the islands, so we just took them."

"The American flag is up, and it must stay there," I said.

"And we'll be involved in another bitter war," she said.

Susan was right. The Filipinos decided to fight. Their leader, **Emilio Aguinaldo**, had been our ally in the war against Spain. Now he became our enemy. Fighting between the rebels led by Aquinaldo and the Americans quickly grew into a

---

People and Terms to Know

Anti-Imperialist League—organization formed in 1898 in Boston whose members were against the United States taking control of the Philippines.

Emilio Aguinaldo—(1869–1964) leader of the Philippine rebels against the Americans. He was captured in 1901 and then pledged his allegiance to the United States.

series of brief, fierce battles that cost American forces 57 dead and 215 wounded.

The fighting dragged on. After nine months, 56,000 American troops had landed in the Philippines. Even though Americans outnumbered them, the Filipinos had the advantage because they knew the country-side and could continue to hide and then attack.

"Since when do we have the right to decide what is best for other people?"

I began to question the war. But politicians like Senator **Henry Cabot Lodge** explained why America should continue to fight: "Manila with its magnificent bay is the prize and pearl of the East. . . . It will keep us open to the markets of China."

President McKinley went further when he vowed to "civilize and Christianize Filipinos."

That comment bothered me, but it made Susan furious.

"Since when do we have the right to decide what is best for other people?" she said. "Filipinos should be able to choose what religion they practice. Who is

---

People and Terms to Know

Henry Cabot Lodge—(1850–1924) Republican senator from Massachusetts (1893–1924) who favored the U.S. purchase of the Philippines and supported the Philippine-American War.

American troops captured these Spanish and Filipino prisoners.

to say that we Americans are so civil? We *bought* the Philippines, as if people can be bought and sold. That sounds a lot like slavery to me!"

I didn't want to admit it, but I agreed with Susan.

The war raged on. We had better weapons, but the Filipinos had great courage. They would not give up. Many of the Filipino soldiers were peasants by day and soldiers by night.

I began to feel great respect for the Filipinos. Thousands of their soldiers and thousands of their **civilians** had been killed, yet they continued to fight.

The Philippine-American War was a terrible war. A **massacre** took place in the small seaside village called Balangiga. The townspeople suddenly attacked 74 American soldiers who were eating breakfast. Within minutes, only 4 of the soldiers were still alive.

When Americans back home heard about the massacre, they wanted revenge. **General "Howling Jake" Smith** ordered his men to kill anybody who could carry a gun, anyone more than 10 years old!

"I want no prisoners," General Smith said. "I wish you to kill and burn; the more you kill and burn, the better you will please me."

When the smoke cleared, the region had been turned into a "howling wilderness." There was nothing left.

Finally, on July 4, 1902, President Theodore Roosevelt declared the Philippine-American War

People and Terms to Know

civilians—people who are not in the military.

massacre—killing of a group of people in an especially cruel way.

General "Howling Jake" Smith—James Francis Smith (1859–1928), U.S. military commander in the Philippine-American War. When he returned to the United States, Smith was court-martialed and convicted.

over. No one will ever know for sure how many Filipino civilians died. Estimates range from 200,000 to one million. Americans lost 4,234 men and suffered another 2,818 wounded.

I joined the Anti-Imperialist League shortly after the war. Never again did I want my country to stop innocent people from being free.

*   *   *

After 425 years of foreign rule—Spanish until 1898, then American—the Philippines gained independence on July 4, 1946. The new government was modeled after that of the United States.

But freedom came with strings attached. The Philippines needed money from America. In exchange for American funds, the president of the Philippines agreed to allow U. S. military bases to remain. He also agreed to limits on trade.

Today, about 2,727,000 Filipinos are American citizens. Filipino Americans hold important political positions from state governor to city mayors and judges. Many others have made their names in sports, entertainment, arts, education, and business. What started so badly has become today a peaceful and important alliance.

QUESTIONS TO CONSIDER

1. What events led to the start of the Spanish-American War?

2. What role did the Treaty of Paris play in relations between the United States and the Philippines?

3. How do you think Emilio Aguinaldo felt after the United States "bought" his country for $20 million?

4. How would you explain why the Anti-Imperialists were against the war in the Philippines?

5. Who would you have sided with during the Philippine-American War and why?

The Panama Canal

BY STEPHEN FEINSTEIN

I looked around the room—and I did not like what I saw. This room didn't look at all like what I had been expecting. When I accepted a job as steam shovel operator on the Panama Canal construction project, this is what I had been promised: clean, decent living quarters—my own room, with a single bed, a mattress, a lamp, two chairs, a dresser, a table, a washstand, and a bowl and pitcher. This is what I got: a filthy unscreened barracks room with only six cots. So I guessed I would have to share "my" room with five other workers.

My name is Richard Anderson, but people call me Rick. In November 1904, I had traveled 2,000 miles by ship, all the way from New York City to Panama. I was excited by the idea of being part of the biggest, most complex construction project in history.

These Spaniards from the region of Galicia were among the workers who

With the expansion of the United States to the west, the demand for a quick, easy route between the East and West coasts had grown. Sailing around South America was costly, time-consuming, and dangerous. In the 1880s, the French had attempted to build a canal across the **Isthmus** of Panama. The French **excavated** part of the route, but their project failed. Now it was America's turn, and I had agreed to help.

✳ ✳ ✳

I had expected that life in the **Panama Canal Zone** would not be easy—tropical heat, bugs, floods—you name it. That was OK with me. But I hadn't guessed the half of it. My roommates trickled in from work as I stashed my things away under my cot. For the most part, these guys seemed friendly, although they didn't look too happy.

My first meal in the company cafeteria with my new roommates was an eye-opener. The food I had been promised—you know, fresh eggs, milk, and

---

People and Terms to Know

Isthmus—narrow strip of land connecting two larger land areas.

excavated—dug.

Panama Canal Zone—strip of territory ten miles wide (five miles on either side of the Panama Canal) granted to the United States by Panama for building and maintaining the Panama Canal. Control of the Zone and Canal was turned over to Panama in 1999.

fruit—was missing. The food that night was almost impossible to eat. No wonder my roommates were less than cheerful. We struggled to swallow the foul-tasting fish on moldy bread. A tall, thin roommate from St. Louis, Ned Coleman, declared, "This food ain't fit for a dog," and he pushed his plate away in disgust.

> *We struggled to swallow the foul-tasting fish on moldy bread.*

My roommates were all Americans. Ned operated another steam shovel. The others worked in offices. Although we complained about our living conditions, others had it much worse. At least two-thirds of the 3,500 workers in the Zone at this time were unskilled black men from the West Indies. They spent their days chopping through the rock with pickaxes in the broiling sun or in the pouring rain. They drilled holes and planted dynamite, blasting any hillside that needed to be moved. For their grueling and dangerous work, they got less than half the wages we made. Still, conditions in the West Indies must have been even worse because they seemed glad to have the work.

I became part of a ten-man crew on a giant, brand-new **Bucyrus steam shovel**. At first, I was happy to be working on such a modern machine. Ned was on the same crew, and he showed me the ropes. The work proved difficult. For weeks, we would shovel hundreds of tons of earth, only to have a **landslide** refill the area we had just excavated. But that was not all. Chief engineer **John Findley Wallace** couldn't organize the work to save his life. Wallace had wisely ordered Bucyrus steam shovels, which were much better than other steam shovels, but he had neglected to provide trains to carry away the dirt and rocks that we excavated. So, much of the time the shovels just sat there. Ned and I eventually received other tasks to do.

The almost daily heavy rains of Panama's rainy season made life miserable during the next few months. The rains caused landslides and did little to ease the thick steamy tropical heat. Adding to the misery were the mosquitoes that seemed to be

---

People and Terms to Know

Bucyrus steam shovel—ninety-five-ton steam shovel capable of taking up five cubic yards (about eight tons) of rock and earth with a single scoop. It was manufactured and sold by the Bucyrus Company.

landslide—fall of a mass of rock and mud.

John Findley Wallace—(1852–1921) appointed chief engineer overseeing the digging of the Panama Canal in 1904, he served less than a year. Although Wallace had a lot of experience building railroads, he seemed to have no plan for the canal project. His best contribution was deciding to use heavy-duty American steam shovels.

▲

Excavating the Culebra Cut was one of the most difficult challenges for those who built the Panama Canal.

everywhere. Barrels and pools of standing water created breeding grounds for these insects.

One day, one of my roommates, Paul Young from Chicago, came back from work and collapsed on his cot. Inside our hot and humid room, Paul could not stop shivering. I felt his forehead. The poor guy was burning up with fever! For the next few days, Paul was constantly thirsty. He complained of splitting headaches. He could not keep food down. Then Paul seemed to get better, except that his skin was turning yellow.

"Oh, my God!" cried Ned. "It's yellow fever!" That night, Paul slipped into a **coma**. By morning he had died. Other workers also caught yellow fever, and many died. Panic spread. Those who could afford it booked passage out of Panama. By the end of March 1905, about three-quarters of the Americans had fled. I myself was tempted to leave.

Panic spread. Those who could afford it booked passage out of Panama.

"Are you gonna run away like the others?" sneered Ned. "Listen, Rick, where else on earth are you gonna have the chance to make history?" In spite of all his complaints about the food and other things, Ned clearly was caught up in the dream of building the canal. That got to me. I decided to take my chances and stay with the project, but not our chief engineer! John Findlay Wallace left in July. **John Frank Stevens** replaced Wallace as chief

---

People and Terms to Know

coma—deep state of unconsciousness, often caused by disease or injury.
John Frank Stevens—(1853–1943) chief engineer of the Panama Canal project who understood the need for organization, food, clean housing, and freedom from disease.

engineer. From day one, Stevens declared that killing off mosquitoes was the top priority.

*   *   *

Dr. William Gorgas, chief of the medical staff in the Zone, knew that those darn mosquitoes were spreading the disease. He said that the yellow fever virus was transmitted by the female *Stegomyia* mosquito. With Stevens' support Dr. Gorgas organized thousands of workers in a huge effort. I would have preferred to operate the shovel but was glad to do my part. We **fumigated** every building in Panama City, Colón, and every other town in the Zone. We supplied all towns with running water. By November 1906, Dr. Gorgas had eliminated yellow fever. Gorgas was not able to totally eliminate malaria in the Zone, but he reduced cases of malaria from 821 per 1,000 people in 1906 to 76 per 1,000 people in 1913. I survived the yellow fever scare, thanks to Doc, and I'm glad that I stayed on.

Stevens turned out to be a business-like, no-nonsense kind of guy. With the health situation under control, he was eager to make up for lost time. He

People and Terms to Know

Dr. William Gorgas—William Crawford Gorgas (1854–1920), American army surgeon and sanitation expert.

fumigated—used smoke or fumes to destroy insects.

brought in thousands of new workers. He also saw to it that our living conditions, including the quality of our food, improved. Stevens told us, "There are three diseases in Panama. They are yellow fever, malaria, and cold feet, and the greatest of these is cold feet."

For reasons unknown to me, Stevens resigned on February 12, 1907, less than two years after his arrival in Panama. In his farewell speech, he said, "You don't need me any longer. All you have to do now is to dig a ditch."

Of course, we knew that things weren't quite that simple. The complicated series of **locks, dams, spillways, and powerhouses** had not yet been designed. A huge earthen dam had to be built to create Gatun Lake. Then there was the major obstacle—the Culebra Cut.

*   *   *

George Goethals, an army colonel, replaced Stevens. Upon his arrival in Panama in March 1907, Goethals announced, "I now consider that I am commanding the Army of Panama, and that the

---

People and Terms to Know

locks, dams, spillways, and powerhouses—working parts of a canal that allow water levels to rise and fall.

George Goethals—George Washington Goethals (1858–1928), American general and engineer who oversaw the completion of the Panama Canal.

enemy we are going to combat is the Culebra Cut and the locks and dams at both ends of the Canal."

We felt lucky to still be alive.

The Culebra Cut was a nine-mile-long channel that had to be dug through a 312-foot-high ridge in the mountains. Work on the Cut began in earnest in 1907.

In 1910, Ned and I were working together on a steam shovel near the bottom of the Culebra Cut. We felt lucky to still be alive. Hundreds had already died in accidents—caught beneath the wheels of trains, struck by flying rock, crushed to death, or blown to bits by dynamite.

Our steam shovel was on a railroad track on a terrace, close to the track of a dirt train. The noise level was head-splitting because of the hundreds of rock drills, the constant blasting, the trains, and the shovel itself. We had to shout just to be heard. So we didn't hear a huge section of the rock wall of the canyon above us when it gave way.

Suddenly, with a monstrous roar, a mass of rock and earth struck our steam shovel. The shovel tipped over like a toy. Standing near an open door, I was thrown clear and flung to the ground. As I got up, dazed, I watched in horror as rock and dirt buried the shovel and the men with it. When the dust settled, only the tip of its crane was showing.

Workers rushed from every direction. We frantically tried to dig out the men buried inside the shovel. It took hours to clear away the boulders. By the time we reached them, all of the men were dead, including my good buddy Ned. That day was probably the luckiest day of my life, but also the saddest day in my life.

On May 20, 1913, the nine-mile-long Culebra Cut, forty feet above sea level from end to end, was finally completed. I was working on Steam Shovel #222. Coming from the opposite direction was Steam Shovel #230. We met on the bottom of the Cut. Everyone climbed down from the shovels. My crew and I jumped up and down like kids. We threw our arms around the men from Steam Shovel #230. Cheers went up from thousands of workers and people looking on.

The following year, on August 15, 1914, the S.S. *Ancon,* a cement carrier, made the first official passage through the Panama Canal. I stood on a hillside above the Culebra Cut, watching the ship far below me. I was filled with pride and wished only that Ned could have been there with me.

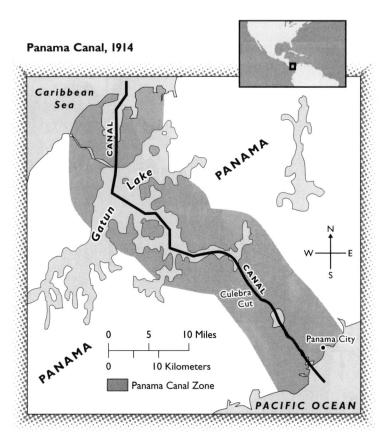

Panama Canal, 1914

Caribbean Sea

CANAL

Gatun Lake

PANAMA

Culebra Cut

CANAL

N
W — E
S

PANAMA

Panama City

0   5   10 Miles

0   10 Kilometers

Panama Canal Zone

PACIFIC OCEAN

QUESTIONS TO CONSIDER

1. Why did Rick Anderson want to help build the Panama Canal?

2. What did Rick expect life to be like in the Panama Canal Zone?

3. According to Dr. Gorgas, what caused the spread of yellow fever?

4. What did John Frank Stevens mean when he said that the greatest disease in Panama was "cold feet"?

5. Why did the United States want to build a canal across Panama?

The Panama Canal
by Elizabeth Mann

Elizabeth Mann's text and Fernando Rangel's colorful and detailed illustrations explain the history and construction of one of the man-made wonders of the world. From Teddy Roosevelt's role in Panama's rebellion for independence in 1903 to the mosquitos and yellow fever that threatened the people working on the canal, this book is an excellent resource for the classroom and independent reader alike.

The Panama Canal
by Barbara Gaines Winkleman

Barbara Gaines Winkleman provides a brief, interesting history of the treaties affecting U.S. control of the canal, the hardships suffered by the Panamanians working on the canal, and the effect the U.S. presence had on the country of Panama itself.

Building the Panama Canal: Chronicles from National Geographic
by Arthur Meier Schlesinger and Fred Israel, editors

Arthur Meier Schlesinger and Fred Israel present a unique perspective on the history of the Panama Canal, focusing on the political and economic aspects of the building of the canal, as well as the effect construction had on humans, plants, and animals.

Sources

Daniel Boone Moves to Kentucky *by Walter A. Hazen*

The narrator and Tom Campbell are fictional characters, but all other characters in the story are historical figures. Sources include *Daniel Boone* by John Mack Faragher (New York: Henry Holt and Company, 1992) and *The American Heritage History of the Great West* by the editors of American Heritage (New York: American Heritage Publishing Co., Inc., 1965).

Constance and the Great Race *by Stephen Currie*

The characters and the steamboat race in this story are fictional. The story's description of river traffic in the late 1800s is historically accurate. For more information, read *Steamboating on the Upper Mississippi* by William J. Petersen (Iowa City, IA: State Historical Society of Iowa, 1937) and *River to the West* by Walter Havighurst (New York: G. P. Putnam's Sons, 1970).

The Trail of Tears *by Diane Wilde*

Etowah is a fictional character. Chief John Ross is a historical figure, and the events described are accurate. Sources include *The Trail of Tears* by Joseph Bruchac (New York: Random House, 1999), *Only the Names Remain—The Cherokees and the Trail of Tears* by Alex W. Bealer (Boston: Little, Brown and Company, 1972), *The Cherokee* by Raymond Bial (New York: Benchmark Books, Marshall Cavendish, 1999), *Trail of Tears—The Rise and Fall of the Cherokee Nation* by John Ehle (New York: Anchor Doubleday, 1988), *Night of the Cruel Moon—Cherokee Removal and the Trail of Tears* by Stanley Hoig (New York: Facts on File, Inc., 1996), *After the Trail of Tears* by William G. McLoughlin (Chapel Hill, NC: University of North Carolina Press, 1993).

Lewis and Clark Meet the Shoshone
by Judith Lloyd Yero

The characters in this story are historic figures, and the events really happened. Several members of the expedition kept journals, and the entries in this story are retellings from their accounts of the trip. A good source for more information about Sacagawea is *Sacagawea of the Lewis and Clark Expedition* by Ella Clark (Berkeley, CA: University of California Press, 1979).

Jim Beckwourth Lives with the Crow *by Danny Miller*

Running Deer is a fictional character, but Chief Big Bowl and Jim Beckwourth are historical figures. This account is based on Jim Beckwourth's experiences during the six years he lived with the Crow Indians. More information about this trailblazing adventurer can be found in his autobiography, *Mountain Man, Indian Chief: The Life and Adventures of Jim Beckwourth*, written from his own dictation by T. D. Bonner and later edited, with a new introduction and epilogue, by Betty Shepard (New York: Harcourt, Brace & World, Inc., 1968).

The Texas Revolution Begins *by Jane Leder*

The narrator and his wife, Mary, are fictional characters. Stephen F. Austin, Noah Smithwick, the Karankawa, Jim Bowie, Sam Houston, and Santa Anna are all historical figures. The events described are historically accurate. The major source for this story is *The Evolution of a State* by Noah Smithwick (Austin: University of Texas Press, 1983).

The Oregon Trail *by Judith Conaway*

Catherine, Justin, and Adela are fictional characters. The other people in the story are historical figures. Sources include *The Commerce of the Prairies* by Josiah Gregg (Santa Barbara, CA: Narrative Press, 2001), *The Oregon Trail: Sketches of Prairie and Rocky Mountain Life* by Francis Parkman (New York: Viking, 1989), and *The Shaping of America: A Geographical Perspective on 500 Years of History, Volume 2: Continental America, 1800–1867* by D.W. Meinig (New Haven: Yale University Press, 1993). Information about Louis Vieux comes from the Kansas Collection (University of Kansas) web site at **http://kuhttp.cc.ukans.edu/carrie/kancoll/gallist.htm**.

The California Gold Rush *by Mary Kathleen Flynn*

Lilly, her husband, and her parents are fictional characters, but Dame Shirley is a historical figure, and the mining town of Rich Bar really existed. The story is based on *The Shirley Letters from the California Mines, 1851–1852* (Berkeley, CA: Heyday Books, 2001) and *The Oxford Companion to United States History* (New York: Oxford University Press, 2001).

The Chisholm Trail *by Brian J. Mahoney*

The cowboy who narrates this story is a fictional character. The story is a fictional account based on the experiences of real cowpunchers such as African American cowboy Nat Love and E. C. "Teddy Blue" Abbot. You can read their exciting firsthand accounts in *Westward Expansion, Primary Sources* (Detroit, MI: UXL, 2001). Another good source of information on the American West is *The New Encyclopedia of the American West* (New Haven, CT: Yale University Press, 1998). Also useful is the web site of the National Cowboy and Western Heritage Museum: **http://www.cowboyhalloffame.org**.

Farming on the Great Plains *by Diane Wilde*

Mary and Frank are fictional characters. The descriptions of life on the Great Plains in the 1880s are historically accurate. Sources include *Best of Dee Brown's West, An Anthology* by Dee Brown, (Santa Fe, NM: Clear Light Publishers, 1998), *The Sod-House Frontier, 1854–1890—A Social History of the Northern Plains from the Creation of Kansas and Nebraska to the Admission of the Dakotas* by Everett Dick (Lincoln, NB: University of Nebraska Press, 1954), *How the Settlers Lived* by George and Ellen Laycock (New York: David McKay Company, Inc., 1980), and *The Way to the West, Essays on the Central Plains* by Elliott West (Albuquerque, NM: University of New Mexico Press, 1995).

The Opening of Japan *by Barbara Littman*

The journalist Charles Malotte is a fictional character, but the people and events he describes were real. Information about the opening of Japan can be found in *The World's Story: A History of the World in Story, Song and Art*, Volume I, *China, Japan, and the Islands of the Pacific* edited by Eva March Tappan (Boston: Houghton Mifflin, 1914).

A Hawaiian Speaks of His Last Queen *by Dee Masters*

The narrator of this story is fictional, but the other characters and the events are historically accurate. Sources include *Shoal of Time: A History of the Hawaiian Islands* by Gavan Daws (Honolulu: The University Press of Hawaii, 1968), *To Steal a Kingdom* by Michael Dougherty (Waimanalo, HI: Island Style Press, 1992), *Hawaii's Story: by Hawaii's Queen* by Lilu'uokalani (Rutland, VT: Charles E. Tuttle Co., 1979), and *Hawaii: A Bicentennial History* by Ruth M. Tabrah (New York: W.W. Norton, 1980).

African-American Troops in Cuba *by Judith Conaway*

Sam, the main character in this story, is fictional, but all the other characters are historical figures. The story describes actual events. The main sources for this story were official reports filed immediately after the battle. The source for Sam's speech at the end of the story is a sermon by the Rev. H.H. Proctor, delivered before the Colored Military Companies of Atlanta, Sunday evening, May 1, 1898, at the First Congregational Church, at the start of the Spanish-American War. For more information, see *Black Jack in Cuba: General John J. Pershing's Service in the Spanish-American War* by Kevin Hymet (pamphlet available on the web site of the Center for Military History: **http://www.army.mil/cmh-pg/documents/spanam/ WS-Prshg.htm**). Other sources include *Eyewitness: The Negro in American History*, 3rd ed., by William Loren Katz (Belmont, CA: Pitman Learning, Inc., 1974), *The Negro and the War* by H.H. Proctor (Atlanta, GA: Mutual Printing Company, 1898) available online from the Daniel A.P. Murray Collection of the Library of Congress, **http://memory.loc.gov/ammem/aap/aaphome.html**. Official Army reports on the actions of the buffalo soldiers at the Battle of Santiago are available at the U.S. Army web site: **http://www.army.mil/cmh-pg**.

The Debate Over the Philippines *by Jane Leder*

Ginny, the narrator, and her friend Susan are fictional characters. President McKinley, the admiral's aide, Emilio Aquinaldo, Mark Twain, General "Howling Jake" Smith, and President Theodore Roosevelt are all historical figures. The Anti-Imperialist League is also factual. Sources include *The Filipino Americans* by Veltisezar Bautista (Midlothian, VA: Bookkaus Publishers) and "The Anti-Imperialist League and the Origins of Filipino-American Oppositional Solidarity" by Jim Zwick (*Amerasia Journal* 24, Summer 1998).

The Panama Canal *by Stephen Feinstein*

Rick Anderson, Ned Coleman, and Paul Young are fictional characters. John Findley Wallace, William Crawford Gorgas, John Frank Stevens, and George Washington Goethals are historical figures, and the events described are historically accurate. Sources include *The Path Between the Seas: The Creation of the Panama Canal, 1870–1914* by David McCullough (New York: Simon and Schuster, 1977), and *Panama Canal: Gateway to the World* by Judith St. George (New York: G.P. Putnam's Sons, 1989).

Glossary of People and Terms to Know

Abilene—city in Kansas from which cattle were shipped east by train.

Absaroka—name that the Crow used for their people and their land.

Aguinaldo, Emilio—(1869–1964) leader of the Philippine rebels against the Americans. He was captured in 1901 and then pledged his allegiance to the United States.

Alamo—old mission in San Antonio, Texas, where Texan heroes were massacred by Santa Anna's forces on March 6, 1836. News of Texans' bravery in the terrible battle gave strength to the cause for Texas independence.

ambush—surprise attack by people who are hidden.

Anti-Imperialist League—organization formed in 1898 in Boston whose members were against the United States taking control of the Philippines.

Austin, Stephen F.—(1793–1836) man considered the founder of the state of Texas.

avenge—get revenge for.

barbarians—people considered by another group to be primitive and without culture.

Battle of Concepción—battle that took place on October 28, 1835, in which Jim Bowie and 90 Texans defeated 450 Mexicans near San Antonio, Texas.

Battle of San Jacinto—battle fought on April 21, 1836, in which forces led by Sam Houston defeated the Mexican forces led by Santa Anna. This battle ended the Texas Revolution and secured Texas independence.

bayoneted—killed by a bayonet, a dagger-like blade attached to the end of a rifle.

Beckwourth, Jim—(1798–1866) African-American frontiersman, trapper, and adventurer.

Blackfoot—Native American people of Montana and southwest Canada.

boiler—engine on a steamboat.

Boone, Daniel—(1734–1820) pioneer and frontiersman famous for exploring Kentucky and blazing the trail that led settlers to the West.

Bowie knives—long knives made famous by Jim Bowie (c. 1796–1836). Bowie was a frontiersman who moved to Texas in 1828 and joined the fight for independence from Mexico. He commanded the volunteer forces at the Alamo and died there.

branding—burning ownership symbols into an animal's hide.

braves—North American Indian warriors.

bridle—harness made up of strap, a bit, and reins, fitted about a horse's head and used to control the animal.

Bucyrus steam shovel—ninety-five-ton steam shovel capable of taking up five cubic yards (about eight tons) of rock and earth with a single scoop. It was manufactured and sold by the Bucyrus Company.

buffalo—oxlike mammal, staple of the Plains Indians' diet.

buffalo soldier—name given by the Plains Indians to African Americans who served in the U.S. Army.

bushwhack—propel a boat by grabbing tree branches along the shore and pulling.

California gold rush—name given to the movement of tens of thousands of people who rushed to the state from all over the world in hopes of making a fortune by finding gold.

chaps—heavy leather coverings worn over trousers by cowhands to protect their legs.

Chatillon, Henri—French hunter, trapper, and guide who came from the St. Louis area. Francis Parkman wrote about him in his book *The Oregon Trail*.

Cherokee—Native American group originally living in the land that now covers parts of the states of Georgia, Alabama, Kentucky, South Carolina, North Carolina, and Tennessee.

Cheyenne—group of Algonquin-speaking North American Indians.

Civil War—(1861–1865) war in the United States between the North (the Union) and the South (the Confederacy).

civilians—people who are not in the military.

claim—piece of land a homesteader takes ownership of; the area of the land is defined by stakes, or pegs, driven into the ground.

Clark, William—(1770–1838) American frontiersman who shared leadership of the expedition to the Pacific Northwest with Meriwether Lewis. Clark rescued the expedition from disaster on several occasions. He was the mapmaker and artist of the expedition. He was later involved in the development of the Missouri Territory.

coma—deep state of unconsciousness, often caused by disease or injury.

consul—official appointed by a government to live in a foreign city and represent his or her government's interests there.

Convention of 1832—meeting that took place in San Felipe, Mexico. Fifty-eight delegates from 16 Texas settlements met and wrote a petition to the Mexican government. Officials of Mexico declared the convention illegal.

Corps of Discovery—(1804–1806) also called the Lewis and Clark Expedition. First U.S. overland expedition to the Pacific coast and back to explore the territories that were part of the Louisiana Purchase.

cow town—town at the end of a cattle trail. This kind of town normally had wild cowboys and lots of ways for them to spend their money.

cowman—man who owned land and cattle.

cowpunching—slang for "cowboy work."

Crockett, Davy—(1786–1836) pioneer, politician, and frontier hero. In 1836, he fought and died at the Alamo.

Crow—American Indian people who lived in the region between the Platte and Yellowstone Rivers.

Cumberland Gap—opening or pass in the Cumberland Mountains where present-day Virginia, Kentucky, and Tennessee meet. It served as the gateway to the West in the late 1800s and early 1900s.

Dame Shirley—pen name of Louisa Clappe, whose letters to her sister in 1851 and 1852 show what life was like in the California gold mines.

diplomats—government representatives.

Dole, Sanford—(1844–1926) American lawyer and political leader in Hawaii. He was born in Honolulu and educated in the U.S. Head of the revolutionary government and president of the Republic of Hawaii, he became the first governor of Hawaii.

downstream—in the direction of the river's current.

Du Sable, Jean-Baptiste-Point—(c. 1750–1818) fur trader from Haiti whose trading post on Lake Michigan later became the city of Chicago. He moved to St. Charles, Missouri, around 1800.

Edo—now Tokyo, Japan's capital.

emigrants—people who leave a country to live in another. (Immigrants are people who come into a country.)

excavated—dug.

expedition—journey taken for exploration or battle.

Fillmore, Millard—U.S. president from 1850 to 1853. He sent Commodore Perry to open trade relations with Japan.

flatboats—squarish flat-bottomed cargo boats without an engine, usually less well-built than keelboats.

ford—shallow place where it is easy to cross a river or stream.

Fort Mandan—fort built by the Lewis and Clark Expedition near the Mandan camp. This is where the expedition spent the winter of 1804–1805.

fumigated—used smoke or fumes to destroy insects.

Goethals, George Washington—(1858–1928) American general and engineer who oversaw the completion of the Panama Canal.

gold fever—desire to get rich quickly from a discovery of gold. The "sickness" spread all over the world like wildfire.

Gonzales—settlement in Texas located where the Guadalupe and San Marcos Rivers meet.

Gorgas, William Crawford—(1854–1920) American army surgeon and sanitation expert who rid the Panama Canal Zone of yellow fever.

granaries—buildings for storing grain.

Guam—largest and southernmost island of the Mariana island group in the Pacific Ocean. Guam is approximately 6,000 miles west of San Francisco.

Henderson, Richard—head of the Transylvania Company.

hold—below-deck storage area of a ship.

Hong Kong—special administrative region of China, formerly a British colony, located in southeast China on the South China Sea.

Houston, Sam—(1793–1863) commander-in-chief of the armies of Texas, whose forces defeated the Mexicans at the Battle of San Jacinto. Houston was elected the first president of the Republic of Texas in 1836. Later, he served as senator from Texas and as the governor of Texas.

ice floes—large, floating fragments of sheet ice.

Independence—town in Missouri near the end of the line for steamboat transportation on the Missouri River.

Indian Removal Act—bill that allowed Federal troops to remove large numbers of Indians from their traditional lands and resettle them in lands farther west.

Iolani Palace—royal residence of Hawaii.

isthmus—narrow strip of land connecting two larger land areas.

Jackson, Andrew—(1767–1845) seventh president of the United States. He served from 1829 to 1837.

Kalakaua, David—(1836–1891) ruler of Hawaii from 1874 to 1891, older brother of Liliuokalani.

Kanagawa—Japanese city where the first treaty between Japan and the United States was signed.

Karankawa—term that includes several Native American groups that lived near the Austin colony in Texas.

Kayama—Kayama Yezaiman, Japanese official chosen by the Shogun to negotiate relations between Japan and Perry on both of Perry's visits.

keelboats—long, slim boats without engines that were used for freight.

Kentucky—land west of the Appalachian Mountains. Originally part of Virginia, Kentucky became a state in 1792.

landslide—fall of a mass of rock and mud.

lei—necklace, usually made of flowers.

Lewis, Meriwether—(1774–1809) leader of the first team of explorers to travel to the Pacific Northwest (1804–1806).

Liliuokalani—(1838–1917) last queen of Hawaii; she ruled from 1891 to 1893.

locks, dams, spillways, and powerhouses—working parts of a canal that allow water levels to rise and fall.

Lodge, Henry Cabot—(1850–1924) Republican senator from Massachusetts (1893–1924) who favored the U.S. purchase of the Philippines and supported the Philippine-American War.

lottery—drawing of lots in which prizes are given to winning numbers or names; also, something decided by chance.

Louisiana Purchase—(1803) agreement by which the United States bought the western half of the Mississippi River basin from France for less than three cents per acre. The purchase doubled the size of the United States.

Mandan—American Plains Indians who spoke the Sioux language. The Mandans were a peaceful people who hunted buffalo and farmed. They lived in the Missouri River Valley near present-day Bismarck, North Dakota.

massacre—killing of a group of people in an especially cruel way.

McKinley, William—(1843–1901) president of the United States from 1896 to 1901. He urged Congress to enter the Spanish-American War and gained the Philippines for the United States as well as control of Cuba.

mine—explosive device used to destroy enemy personnel or equipment, often designed to be set off by contact.

Minitari—(also called Hidatsa and Gros Ventres of the Missouri) American Plains Indian people of Sioux descent who lived on the upper Missouri River.

missionaries—people who come into a country to do religious or charity work.

missionary party—political leaders of the settlers in Hawaii. These were mostly Americans whose parents had been missionaries.

moccasins—soft leather slippers worn by American Indians.

Mormons—members of the Church of Jesus Christ of Latter-day Saints; they founded Salt Lake City in 1847.

most favored nation—country with the best trading terms the importing nation gives. Imports from countries named "most favored nation" are taxed less heavily than goods from other countries.

Natchez—Mississippi River port north of New Orleans.

Nebraska—state in the central United States, in the Great Plains.

New England—section of the northeastern United States that includes the states of Maine, New Hampshire, Vermont, Massachusetts, Connecticut, and Rhode Island.

Paducah—Ohio River port in western Kentucky.

Panama Canal Zone—strip of territory ten miles wide (five miles on either side of the Panama Canal) granted to the United States by Panama for building and maintaining the Panama Canal. Control of the Zone and Canal was turned over to Panama in 1999.

Perry, Matthew—(1794–1858) commander of the U.S. fleet that opened Japan to trade with the United States in 1854.

Pershing, J. J.—John Joseph Pershing (1860–1948), white U.S. army officer nicknamed "Black Jack" for his pride in his black troops. He served in Cuba and the Philippines, and later, in World War I, he commanded American forces in Europe.

petitions—formal letters of request signed by many people.

Philippines—country in southeast Asia made up of more than 7,000 islands in the South China and Philippine Seas.

Platte River—river in southern Nebraska.

pole—use a long pole to move a boat by pushing off the river bottom.

Potawatomi—Native American people of the Algonquin language group. In the 1600s, they lived in what is now Wisconsin. They expanded into what is now Michigan, Indiana, and Illinois. In the early 1800s they were forced to sell their land to the U.S. Most moved to a reservation in southern Kansas.

Powhatan—sailing vessel in Commodore Perry's squadron that was used as the meeting and banquet area during Perry's trip to Japan.

prairie—wide, flat, largely treeless grasslands, such as the Great Plains of central North America.

Preble, George Henry—(1816–1885) lieutenant on Perry's expedition to Japan. His letters to his wife provide an excellent record of the mission.

provision—clause or passage in a document or agreement.

Puerto Rico—islands between the Caribbean Sea and North Atlantic Ocean, east of the Dominican Republic. Puerto Rico is about 1,000 miles southeast of Miami, Florida.

quiver—portable case for arrows.

Roosevelt, Theodore—(1858–1919) writer, cowboy, soldier, and politician, Roosevelt got most of the credit for the victory at San Juan Hill in the war against Spain. He served as governor of New York and as vice president under President William McKinley. When McKinley was assassinated in 1901, Roosevelt became president at the age of 42. He served as the 26th U.S. president until 1909.

Ross, John—(1790–1866) most important Cherokee chief at the time of forced removal to Indian Territory in Oklahoma. He was chief of the united Cherokee nation until he died.

Rough Riders—popular nickname of the First Volunteer Cavalry, led by Theodore Roosevelt.

Sacagawea (sah•kah•juh•WAY•ah)—(c. 1786–1812) Shoshone woman who, carrying her infant son on her back, traveled thousands of wilderness miles with the Lewis and Clark Expedition. She acted as translator for the group with the Shoshone and provided the expedition with edible fruits and vegetables. Sacagawea means "Bird Woman."

saloon—drinking establishment.

samurai—member of the military class of Japan. Japanese warriors were expected to be scholars as well as soldiers. They organized the work of the farming, artisan, and merchant classes in Japan.

Santa Anna, Antonio López de—(1794–1876) president of Mexico who led the Mexican forces against the Texans. He was captured at the Battle of San Jacinto but was allowed to return to Mexico.

Santa Fe Trail—trading route between Independence, Missouri, and Santa Fe, New Mexico.

Santiago Bay—harbor in Santiago, Cuba.

scalps—skins covering the top of the head, cut away from an enemy as a battle trophy.

Sequoyah (sih•KWOY•uh)—(c.1770–1843) Cherokee leader who created a new alphabet, which he called "talking leaves," so that Cherokee could read and write their own language.

Shimoda and Hakodate—two of the first Japanese port towns to be opened to American ships that needed supplies and fuel.

Shogun—true ruler of Japan at the time of Perry's missions. The Emperor was only a ceremonial figure. The word *Shogun* means "barbarian-expelling general" in Japanese.

Shoshone (shoh•SHOH•nee)—(also spelled Shoshoni) North American Indian group that once occupied the territory from southeastern California across Nevada and northwestern Utah into southern Idaho and western Wyoming.

Sierra Nevada—mountain range in California where gold was first discovered in the state.

sinkholes—natural depressions in the land surface.

six-shooters—handguns that can fire six bullets without reloading.

Smith, "Howling Jake"—James Francis Smith (1859–1928), U.S. military commander in the Philippine-American War. When he returned to the United States, Smith was court-martialed and convicted.

Smithwick, Noah—(1808–1899) early Texas pioneer. He wrote a book called *The Evolution of a State* (1900). In his book, he paints a clear picture of what life was like at that exciting time in Texas history.

snipers—hidden riflemen.

sod house—house made from chunks of earth and straw.

Spanish-American War—(1898) short war between the United States and Spain. The war began over Cuba, but spread to Puerto Rico, Guam, and the Philippines as well. The U.S. acquired all these islands after the war.

spurs—metal prongs attached to the back of riding boots. They are used to urge the horse forward.

St. Charles—old trading town in Missouri, just north of St. Louis, located where the Missouri, Mississippi, and Illinois Rivers meet.

stampede—group of animals running out of control.

Stevens, John Frank—(1853–1943) chief engineer of the Panama Canal project who understood the need for organization, food, clean housing, and freedom from disease.

Stevens, John L.—(1820–1895) U.S. minister to Hawaii who helped overthrow Queen Liliuokalani by recognizing the revolutionary government and requesting U.S. troops to protect U.S. citizens and property.

stockade—fence of wooden stakes built for defense.

Tasmanian—native of Tasmania, island state of southeast Australia.

tenderfoot—newcomer to the cowboy life.

Tenth United States Cavalry—one of four regiments of African-American soldiers in the U.S. Army. All four regiments of "buffalo soldiers" fought at Santiago, Cuba, during the Spanish-American War.

Texas Revolution—(1835–1836) war that began with the Battle of Gonzales and ended in victory for the Texans at the Battle of San Jacinto.

tipi—cone-shaped Indian shelter made by stretching animal skins over poles.

Trail Boss—boss of a cattle drive.

Transylvania Company—company founded for the purpose of buying land from the Cherokee and establishing Kentucky as the fourteenth colony. The attempt failed.

trappers—people whose occupation is trapping animals, such as beavers, and selling their pelts, or furs.

Treaty of Guadalupe Hidalgo (GWAHD•uh•LOO•pay ih•DAHL•goh)— formal agreement that ended the Mexican-American War in February 1848, and gave the territories of New Mexico, Arizona, California, Utah, and Nevada to the United States.

upstream—against the river's current.

Vieux, Louis—(1809–1872) tribal leader of the Potawatomi Indians and a businessman. He operated trading posts in various places before settling on the Vermilion River. He owned the town site of Louisville, Kansas, which bears his name. He was widely respected for his generosity, public spirit, and honesty.

Walker, John—African-American soldier from Troop D, Tenth U.S. Cavalry. He received the Congressional Medal of Honor for his part in the July 1, 1898, battle in Cuba during the Spanish-American War.

Wallace, John Findley—(1852–1921) appointed chief engineer overseeing the digging of the Panama Canal in 1904, he served less than a year. Although Wallace had a lot of experience building railroads, he seemed to have no plan for the canal project. His best contribution was deciding to use heavy-duty American steam shovels.

Whitman, Marcus—(1802–1847) American missionary and Oregon pioneer.

yellow fever—highly infectious tropical disease that is spread by mosquito bites.

Young, Hiram—freed slave who used his skills in wagon-building, wheel-making, and trading to become one of the wealthiest citizens of Independence, Missouri.

Acknowledgements

9 Courtesy of the Library of Congress.

11 Charles M. Russell, *Lewis and Clark on the Lower Columbia,* opaque and transparent watercolor over graphite underdrawing on paper, 1905. 1961.195. © Amon Carter Museum, Fort Worth, Texas.

16, 19, 20 Courtesy of the Library of Congress.

22 Courtesy of the National Archives.

29 © Metropolitan Museum of Art.

34 © The Filson Club.

37, 41 Courtesy of the Library of Congress.

49, 59 © Woolaroc Museum, Bartlesville, Oklahoma.

63 © E.S. Paxson, Montana Historical Society.

68, 69, 76, 81 Courtesy of the Library of Congress.

84 Courtesy of the Montana Historical Society, photograph by Don Beatty.

87, 94, 96, 98 Courtesy of the Library of Congress.

109 © California State Library, Sacramento.

112, 118, 120, 124, 129, 132, 139, 144, 153, 159 Courtesy of the Library of Congress.

162 Courtesy of the National Archives.

168, 172, 177, 182, 186, 193 Courtesy of the Library of Congress.